Hacik Gazer, Markus Iff, Werner Klän,
Dorothea Sattler (Eds.)

Reconciliation in Remembrance of Jesus Christ

Ökumenische Studien
Ecumenical Studies

herausgegeben von

Prof. Dr. Ulrich Becker
(Hannover)

Prof. Dr. Erich Geldbach
(Bochum)

Prof. Dr. Rebekka Klein
(Bochum)

Prof. Dr. Ulrike Link-Wieczorek
(Oldenburg)

Prof. Dr. Gottfried Orth
(Braunschweig/Rothenburg)

Prof. Dr. Konrad Raiser
(Genf/Berlin)

Prof. Dr. Dorothea Sattler
(Münster)

Band / Volume 53

LIT

Reconciliation in Remembrance of Jesus Christ

Treating Holy Communion, Eucharist and Holy Sacrifice
with Ecumenical Sensitivity

A contribution to the 11th assembly of the WCC
(Karlsruhe, August 2022)

edited by

Hacik Gazer, Markus Iff, Werner Klän,
Dorothea Sattler

LIT

English translation: Neville Williamson

The cover picture and several pictures in the book are by the artist Beatrix Claßen (* 1940) from Mühlheim/Ruhr.

This book is printed on acid-free paper.

Bibliographic information published by the Deutsche Nationalbibliothek
The Deutsche Nationalbibliothek lists this publication in the Deutsche Nationalbibliografie; detailed bibliographic data are available on the Internet at http://dnb.dnb.de.

ISBN 978-3-643-91510-8 (pb)
ISBN 978-3-643-35196-8 (PDF)

A catalogue record for this book is available from the British Library.

© LIT VERLAG GmbH & Co. KG Wien,
Zweigniederlassung Zürich 2022
Flössergasse 10
CH-8001 Zürich
Tel. +41 (0) 76-632 84 35
E-Mail: zuerich@lit-verlag.ch   https://www.lit-verlag.ch
Distribution:
In the UK: Global Book Marketing, e-mail: mo@centralbooks.com
In North America: Independent Publishers Group, e-mail: orders@ipgbook.com
In Germany: LIT Verlag Fresnostr. 2, D-48159 Münster
Tel. +49 (0) 2 51-620 32 22, Fax +49 (0) 2 51-922 60 99, e-mail: vertrieb@lit-verlag.de

Table of Contents

1 Thematic introduction and thanks. 1
2 Forewords from the Ecumenical Community 9
   2.1 Faith and Order Commission of the WCC (Rev. Dr Susan Durber). 9
   2.2 Committee of the host churches for the WCC Assembly (Bishop Petra Bosse-Huber) 11
   2.3 Council of Churches in Germany (Archpriest Radu Constantin Miron). 13
3 Ecumenical theological insights. 17
   (Hacik Gazer, Markus Iff, Werner Klän and Dorothea Sattler)
   3.1 Spiritual ecumenism in the context of other approaches to ecumenism. 17
   3.2 The common confession of Jesus Christ as the basis of ecumenical action 18
   3.3 Convergences achieved in the area of Holy Communion, Eucharist and Holy Sacrifice 20
      3.3.1 Holy Communion and Eucharist – a "sacrifice"? 20
      3.3.2 True presence of Jesus Christ in the meal (Real Presence). 21
   3.4 Connecting the meaning with the form of the liturgy 24
      3.4.1 Liturgical reforms are now made in the ecumenical context 24
      3.4.2 The meaning of the Holy Communion and the Eucharist is the celebration of the paschal mystery . . . 25

		3.4.3 The weekly rhythm	26
		3.4.4 The aim is active participation of all in the liturgies . .	27
		3.4.5 The experience of church communion is effected by the Holy Spirit	29
		3.4.6 Unity in legitimate diversity is to be shaped	30
	3.5	Church communion and communion at the eucharistic meal. .	31

4 Exemplary selected ecumenical dialogues 34
(Hacik Gazer, Markus Iff, Werner Klän and Dorothea Sattler)

    4.1 Multilateral: Declaration of Convergence on the topic of "Eucharist" (Faith and Order, Lima 1982). 35

    4.2 Bilateral dialogues in selection 47

        4.2.1 Anglican / Roman Catholic: clarifications on their statements 47

        4.2.2 Free church and Roman Catholic. 48

        4.2.3 Lutheran/Roman Catholic. 53

        4.2.4 Oriental Orthodox/Roman Catholic 56

        4.2.5 Orthodox/Roman Catholic 60

        4.2.6 Reformed/Roman Catholic 64

        4.2.7 Independent Evangelical Lutheran Church in ecumenical dialogues 65

    4.3 Lutheran, Reformed and United Churches in Europe: "Leuenberg Agreement" (1973) 67

    4.4 Ecumenical Working Group of Protestant and Catholic Theologians (ÖAK): "Together at the Lord's Table" 69

5 Holy Communion – Eucharist – Holy Sacrifice
Joint Statement of the German Ecumenical Study Committee
(DÖSTA) 77

6 "Come and see!"
A concern of the 3rd Ecumenical Kirchentag 2021 in Frankfurt . . 87
Julia Meister und Christoph Stender

    6.1 A look back at the Third Ecumenical Kirchentag (ÖKT). . . . 87

    6.2 Witness of ÖKT 3 92

7 Denominational liturgical traditions
Illustrated by way of example with reference to Sunday, 4
September 2022 93
   7.1 Old Catholic Church (Joachim Pfützner) 93
   7.2 Anglican Church (Christopher Easthill) 105
   7.3 Armenian Apostolic Church (Hacik Gazer) 111
   7.4 Federation of Pentecostal Churches (Frank Uphoff) 117
   7.5 Evangelical Churches in the EKD (Julia Meister). 126
   7.6 Evangelical Lutheran Church in Baden (João Carlos
       Schmidt) 132
   7.7 United Methodist Church (Annette Gruschwitz and Thomas
       Roscher) 135
   7.8 Orthodox Churches (Marina Kiroudi) 144
   7.9 Roman Catholic Church (Christoph Stender) 150

8 Diversity of liturgies – a brief overview 156
(Hacik Gazer, Markus Iff, Werner Klän and Dorothea Sattler)
   8.1 Formation of liturgical traditions in East and West 156
   8.2 Service reform 157
       8.2.1   Reforms in the realm of Protestant churches 157
       8.2.2   Reforms in the realm of the Roman Catholic Church. . 159

9 Suggestions for an ecumenically sensitive liturgical practice. . . . 161
   9.1 Basic thoughts 161
   9.2 Practical examples. 162
       9.2.1   Participation of members of the congregation. 162
       9.2.2   Selection of songs 162
       9.2.3   Liturgy of the Word 162
       9.2.4   Creed, Lord's Prayer and Blessing 163
       9.2.5   Intercessory prayer 163
       9.2.6   Ecumenically sensitive design of the meal celebration . 163
       9.2.7   Commemoration of the dead 164
       9.2.8   Respect for the ordained ministry and special
           ministries. 164

9.2.9 Baptism and Holy Communion, Eucharist and Holy Sacrifice 165
9.2.10 Eucharistic Liturgy and Agape 166

10 Authors 168

1 Thematic introduction and thanks

1.1 Thematic introduction

Since 24 February 2022, many of us who have long been involved in Christian ecumenism have been at a loss for words to interpret what is happening. Wartime has broken out in Ukraine. In their hostility to one another, even baptised Christians are killing on both sides. Christians are united in their celebration of Easter hope, but the fighting did not even stop at this festival time. Interests that have nothing to do with religion are once again, as before, determining the actions of nations. We are experiencing destructive violence on a scale and in a form that we no longer expected in our neighbourhood in Europe. At the same time, we observe the many other places in the world where people are suffering from armed conflicts: in Syria, Yemen, Afghanistan, Nigeria, Israel and Palestine. And there are many other places where the violence escapes our notice. Christians all over the world are deeply saddened by all the suffering; we gather to pray for peace, struggle for diplomatic solutions – yet we often experience ourselves as powerless. It is true: we do not know how we should pray. Our common hope is Jesus Christ. He is our peace (Eph 2:14).

As an informal study group in the German-speaking multilateral ecumenical community without any official church commission, we would like to face the current challenges described above and take the opportunity to help the 11th Assembly of the World Council of Churches in Karlsruhe 2022 to reflect on common eucharistic spirituality. The opportunity is favourable, because the Council of Christian Churches in Germany (ACK) is at present conducting an intensive multilateral ecumenical discussion on this topic. Many people still recall the national Ecumenical Kirchentag 2021 in Frankfurt am Main, which strengthened the hopes of a common eucharistic witness in the world.

1 Thematic introduction and thanks

The 3rd Ecumenical Kirchentag in Germany – jointly organised by the Central Committee of German Catholics (ZdK) and the German Protestant Kirchentag (DEKT) – has made us increasingly aware of an issue that was already important at the previous Ecumenical Kirchentags: the strengthening of multilateral ecumenism. During the first of these events in Berlin in 2003, the focus lay on the one baptism and on the affirmation of the Charta Oecumenica (ChOe), which had been signed at the European level in Strasbourg on 22 April 2001. On the occasion of the 2nd Ecumenical Kirchentag 2010 in Munich, an agreement was reached on the annual organisation of a Season of Creation from 1 September to 4 October; moreover, the liturgy of the breaking of bread following vespers in the Orthodox liturgical rite (artoklasia) strengthened the hope that we may once share a eucharistic meal together in Christian solidarity. In the Charta Oecumenica, all church leaders in Europe commit themselves "in the power of the Holy Spirit, to work towards the visible unity of the Church of Jesus Christ in the one faith, expressed in the mutual recognition of baptism and in eucharistic fellowship, as well as in common witness and service." (ChOe 1)[1].

In these difficult times, we here present a study intended as a small contribution to the search for reconciliation between the denominations. May reconciliation in remembrance of Jesus Christ be experienced through ecumenically sensitive forms of the liturgical celebrations of the Holy Communion, Eucharist and Holy Sacrifice. People with a high respect for the Christian ecumenical movement are nowadays unceasingly conscious of Jesus' prayer and sustain the longing for a common eucharistic meal in his memory. "Do this in remembrance of me" (1 Cor 11:24). These words of Jesus, handed down by Paul, are connected with a promise: Jesus' commission is fulfilled in the sharing of the one loaf and the drinking from the one cup. In these two symbolic acts, Jesus interprets his life as an expression of God's unconditional covenantal will and his unlimited preparedness for reconciliation.

After long periods of controversy, ecumenical discussions have now led to many convergences on the theological meaning and the appropriate liturgical form of celebration. In this context, the convergence statements of the Faith and Order Commission on the topics of "Baptism, Eucharist

---

[1] Conference of European Churches and Council of European Bishops' Conferences (eds.), Charta Oecumenica. Guidelines for the Growing Cooperation among the Churches in Europe, St. Gallen / Geneva 2001.

and Ministry" (Lima 1982) are still of significant influence today.² It is noticeable that since this document the topic of Eucharist, Holy Communion and Holy Sacrifice has receded into the background in the international multilateral ecumenical context, and thus in the interdenominational dialogues.

In many bilateral dialogues over the decades, the topics of Holy Communion, Eucharist and Holy Sacrifice have been repeatedly mentioned. In the land of the Reformation, Germany, a study by the Ecumenical Working Group of Protestant and Catholic Theologians entitled "Together at the Lord's Table"³ has aroused great interest. The study's theologically based plea for participation in the liturgical celebrations of other denominations, trusting in the presence of Jesus Christ in the Holy Spirit, has also been critically received.⁴ At the same time, this dialogue has given new impetus to an intensified effort towards a common understanding and an ecumenically sensitive practice of Holy Communion, Eucharist and Holy Sacrifice in the worldwide Christian community.

We are convinced that this topic needs to be revisited today under new auspices: at times which emphasise the "ecumenism of gifts", spiritual approaches to the Christian faith are held in high esteem. The diversity of liturgies in remembrance of Jesus Christ is respected. The gathering of believers who trust in the presence of Jesus Christ provides a very important witness to faith. God's Spirit makes Jesus Christ effectively present. Eucharist, diakonia and witness in the world are seen to be closely connected with each other.

As colleagues, as brothers and sisters who know one another well in multilateral ecumenism, we have undertaken to report on the state of understanding reached in ecumenical dialogues worldwide. Open questions are named. Indications are given as to how ecumenical sensitivity can be promoted in spite of separate denominational liturgies. Information is given

---

[2] Faith and Order Commission of the World Council of Churches, Declaration of Convergence on "Baptism, Eucharist and Ministry" (Lima 1982)

[3] Cf. Volker Leppin / Dorothea Sattler (eds.), Together at the Lord's Table. A statement by the Ecumenical Working Group of Protestant and Catholic Theologians, Freiburg / Göttingen 2020 (bilingual edition in German and English).

[4] Cf. Volker Leppin / Dorothea Sattler (eds.). Gemeinsam am Tisch des Herrn. Ein Votum des Ökumenischen Arbeitskreises evangelischer und katholischer Theologen, Vol. II: Anliegen und Rezeption, Freiburg / Göttingen 2021.

on the liturgical orders of service and the lectionaries prescribed in individual traditions. Taking the example of the confessional liturgies foreseen for Sunday, 4 September 2022, during the Assembly of the World Council of Churches, one can recognise which prayers and songs can be spoken and sung together in all denominations. Getting to know how eucharistic services will take place liturgically on this day all over the world is highly significant for confessional studies. Strengthening ecumenical sensitivity in thinking and celebrating is very beneficial on the path towards a joint celebration of Holy Communion, Eucharist and Holy Sacrifice in remembrance of Jesus Christ. A selection of source texts from ecumenical dialogues can provide insights into the ecumenical knowledge already gained on the subject.

A number of suggestions for going into the subject more deeply, together with thematic overviews and illustrations, may well be helpful as we attempt to take practical steps in Christian churches all over the world and, if possible, in the near future, in order to share with one another our experiences in eucharistic services or other forms of worship. In the framework of educational work and in ecumenical fellowship, whether in small groups or larger discussions, we could let one another know what the celebration of the Holy Communion, Eucharist and Holy Sacrifice means to baptised Christians in their everyday lives. We still know far too little about each other. We are just getting to know each other. We can share our spirituality and answer specific questions as we speak to one another. When did I first celebrate Holy Communion, Eucharist or Holy Sacrifice? What hope and strength do these liturgies give me in daily life? Which worship services have left a lasting impression in my memory? What part of the liturgical form is sacred to me? How can I express in words my experience of the presence of Jesus Christ? What commission accompanies me into my life after leaving the service?

The positive experiences made during the 3rd Ecumenical Kirchentag in dealing sensitively with the subject of the Holy Communion, Eucharist and Holy Sacrifice motivated us to call out to the world in Jesus' words: "Come and see!" (Jn 1:39). Jesus invites those he has called to experience his presence in the flesh. The joint remembrance of Jesus' mission unites us. At the same time, we are aware of the difference between the temporal dawning of the Kingdom of God on earth and the expectation of the parousia of Jesus Christ in eschatological perfection.

The churches have different rules and regulations with regard to the joint celebration of the Holy Communion, Eucharist and Holy Sacrifice across denominational borders. Beyond the question of when the hope will be fulfilled that we will one day celebrate the memory of Jesus Christ together at the Lord's Table in reconciled fellowship, we can be spiritually enriched by paying attention to the diversity of liturgical forms of celebration. As believers in Christ we listen together to God's Word, which teaches us: "In Christ God was reconciling the world to himself, not counting their trespasses against them, and entrusting the message of reconciliation to us. So we are ambassadors for Christ, since God is making his appeal through us; we entreat you on behalf of Christ, be reconciled to God." (2 Cor 5:19-20).

1.2 Thanks

As editors and publishers of this study, we would like to thank all those who contributed to it as authors.

The concept of this study has been developed on the personal initiative of an informal circle of people with ecumenical experience. Apart from those mentioned by name in the study, these include: Dr Jörg Bickelhaupt, Dr Michael Kappes, Dr Johannes Oeldemann, Bishop Emmanuel Sfiatkos and Dr Marc Witzenbacher. Dr Simone Sinn was very helpful in the contact with Faith and Order.

With regard to the present publication, valuable support was provided both by Alina Mielke, who took the minutes in the informal circle of those bringing in ideas, as well as by Jan-Hendrik Mönch, who prepared the printed version. Without the uncomplicated and invariably focused consultations with the editor from the LIT publishing house, Dr Michael J. Rainer, this publication could not have been produced in such a short time.

Our special thanks go to the artist Beatrix Classen (*1940) from Mülheim an der Ruhr, who allowed us to choose from the rich treasury of her works those that underlined our interest. Interruptions can stimulate reflection – maybe also when sketching out ecumenical learning paths by looking at pictures together. Theses pictures have not been chosen arbitrarily: over and over again, the motif of the cross shines out, reminding us of Jesus' death. All churches celebrate this mystery of faith: in death there is life. Some of the pictures remind us with circles and spirals of the lively movement that is so important in ecumenism. Abstractions allow associations and lead to a sharing of perceptions. The theme of one of the pictures is clearly identifiable. It is the first one in the book and should be considered before delving into the collection of our ecumenical insights. Here we can recognise in modern terms a motif which is well-known since the early days of Christian theology. The revelation of the nature and the name of God at the burning bush (cf. Ex 3:14) is made real in time and history in the incarnation of God in Jesus Christ. As the "image of the invisible God" (Col 1:15), Jesus let us experience who God is: a faithful, just and merciful being. The remembrance of Jesus Christ forms the centre of the Christian confession. The child Jesus lives for a short period and dies on the thorny cross. In the fire of the Holy Spirit, Jesus Christ is recognised and continues to work in our memory.

May it come true again in our lifetimes: "Christ's love moves the world to reconciliation and unity." This motto of the 11th Assembly of the World Council of Churches is a challenge in these months in which we are preparing to host the ecumenical world in Germany – in our country, which is persistently aware of its own history of guilt and is grateful that the weapons of war aimed at one another in the world were finally laid down on 8 May 1945.

Erlangen, Ewersbach, Lübeck and Münster, on 8 May 2022

Hacik Gazer, Markus Iff, Werner Klän and Dorothea Sattler

2 Forewords from the Ecumenical Community

2.1 Faith and Order Commission of the WCC (Rev. Dr Susan Durber)

I write with heartfelt appreciation of this initiative to bring the theme of eucharistic communion to the centre of ecumenical conversation. Informal initiatives like this are often precisely the place where the more formal ecumenical movement is reminded of its very mission.

From the very beginning of the Faith and Order movement, a movement that later became part of the WCC, the goal of visible unity was expressed in terms of fellowship at the Lord's table. The mission of the Faith and Order Commission is still expressed today as follows:

"The primary purpose of the Faith and Order Commission is to serve the churches as they call one another to visible unity in one faith and in one eucharistic fellowship expressed in worship and common life in Christ, through witness and service to the world, and go forth towards that unity that the world may believe." (Constitution of the Faith and Order Commission).

The most valued text of the Faith and Order Commission, *Baptism, Eucharist and Ministry*, was published in 1982, accompanied by the *Lima Liturgy*, a eucharistic text intended to express in liturgical form the convergence in the theology and practice of the Eucharist. In many ecumenical and also local church contexts, I have enjoyed participating in celebrations that express this convergence and I have used the liturgy. Before the end of the last millennium, I attended a conference on the Isle of Iona which was marked by the hope that by the year 2000 we would be able to celebrate the Eucharist together at the Lord's Table. It seems amazing when I look back now and realise that this was perceived as a realistic hope at the time. However, such hopes for the fullest expression of visible unity within "our lifetime" have faded somewhat, and the focus of ecclesiological ecumenism has shifted to other issues: diversity in moral issues, synodality, the role of the laity, and others. While these new questions are vital in themselves, we have paid too little attention to the possibility or hope of celebrating the Eucharist together. This is despite the fact that, ironically, we have indeed found a degree of convergence in our understanding of the Eucharist. I have taught as a lecturer in the ecumenical seminars how to prepare and celebrate a liturgy of the Holy Communion based on the insights of *Baptism, Eucharist and Ministry*. But we still celebrate separately and don't seem to find another way.

I welcome the multilateral initiative of the group of theologians from different church traditions in Germany who have been reflecting on what ecumenically sensitive liturgies of the Holy Communion might look like. Such liturgies are important on the journey, keeping alive the passion for the vision of eucharistic communion. Their efforts remind us all of the hope for visible unity expressed around Christ's table.

And indeed, their work reflects the many voices of those who today seek an ecumenism that finds its home in the "in-between" space of theological dialogue and common action – in common spirituality and common prayer. Such voices were evident in the churches' responses to the Faith and Order Commission's recent convergence text, *The Church: Towards a Common Vision* (2013). Those involved in this project in Germany are reading the signs of the times and setting before us an ecumenism that asks what gifts we each bring to ecumenical togetherness and bring to the table, and how we can truly imagine a common Eucharist. They do this work for the Church of Jesus Christ, and they deserve our gratitude. May their work bear fruit as we seek ways to animate and keep alive the ecumenical movement through informal and passionate initiatives like these and in its more formal and representative institutions.

At the 11th Assembly of the WCC we will gather under the theme "The love of Christ moves, reconciles and unites the world". Let us never forget the power of Christ's love to move *the Church* and to call us to gather together to celebrate the eucharistic feast. I am grateful for all those who are preparing seriously and carefully for this festive day.

Rev. Dr Susan Durber

2.2 Committee of the host churches for the WCC Assembly (Bishop Petra Bosse-Huber)

When the WCC holds its Assembly in Germany in 2022 for the first time in the history of the ecumenical movement, it will be confronted with a special ecumenical situation. Ecumenical cooperation in Germany is mostly the domain of the Roman Catholic and Protestant churches. In addition, the question of joint participation at Holy Communion or the Eucharist is being raised more and more urgently among church-goers. Before this goal can be reached, several steps must still be taken and a number of questions solved. But much has already been achieved on this path. At the international level, this includes above all the text of the Faith and Order Commission "Baptism, Eucharist and Ministry" from 1982. This declaration was able to clear up former conflicts concerning the presence of Christ and the understanding of sacrifice. It also aimed at a greater degree of eucharistic communion between the churches. In the German context, the statement "Together at the Lord's Table" was published in 2020 by the Ecumenical Working Group of Protestant and Catholic Theologians (ÖAK). Against the background of the understandings already achieved, it calls on the one hand for a strengthening of the mutual understanding of the respective traditions, and recommends on the other hand that the meal of each denomination be celebrated in a form that is ecumenically sensitive.

The Council of the Evangelical Church in Germany (EKD) commended this statement as a further theologically consistent stage on the common path that the Protestant and Roman Catholic churches, together with other denominations, had taken in 2007 with their mutual recognition of baptism. In 2007, eleven of the then 17 member churches of the Council of Churches in Germany had signed a mutual recognition of baptism.[1] The signatory churches explicitly referred to the text of the Faith and Order Commission from 1982, understanding their agreement on baptism as a consistent continuation of the Lima statement. The Council of the EKD considered the ÖAK statement, which was itself based on these two texts, a constructive perspective that could lead to a theologically responsible

---

[1] The text of the declaration can be found at https://www.oekumene-ack.de/fileadmin/user_upload/Themen/Taufanerkennung2007.pdf (02.05.2022). On the origins, cf. Karl Heinz Voigt, Ökumene in Deutschland. Von der Gründung der ACK bis zur Charta Oecumenica (1948 to 2001), Göttingen 2015, 625f.

deepening of ecumenical fellowship. The Council was particularly grateful for the analysis of the witness of Holy Scripture. For the reference to the common basis of the different traditions makes it clear that "the diversity of the different traditions does not mean arbitrariness but richness"[2]. The Council expressed the hope that further discussion of the text would allow its promising potential to bear fruit.

I am therefore very grateful that theologians from multilateral ecumenism have taken the initiative in putting together this collection of material in order to contribute to this topic in connection with the 2022 Assembly of the World Council of Churches. This booklet does not only present a concise compilation of the issues and possible solutions that have so far been discussed regarding the Holy Communion, the Eucharist and Holy Sacrifice, as well as the results during the multilateral academic debate in the German Ecumenical Study Committee and the preparations for the 3rd Ecumenical Kirchentag 2021 in Frankfurt; in addition, it summarises the traditions of the churches in a very practical way, paving the way for possible forms of eucharistic celebration which are ecumenically sensitive and strive towards unity. This is combined with the proposal and hope that many of the services celebrated during the Assembly, not only in Karlsruhe but also in many other places, will draw on these traditions, and that this will encourage the development of an ecumenically sensitive practice in the future.

It is my personal hope that the WCC Assembly 2022 in Karlsruhe will make multilateral ecumenism in Germany and Europe more visible in the long term, so that one will perceive more clearly the great diversity of denominations already living and working together here. I am hoping that there will be a significant impetus for our ecumenical situation in Europe and in Germany. We often have the feeling that we have already clarified a great deal from the theological point of view, but that we do not yet dare to draw the consequences on a practical level. The Assembly and its witness for a strengthening unity could help us to be more consistent and courageous as we live together ecumenically on the local level. This also involves taking confident, yet responsible and ecumenically sensitive steps towards more visible unity, including the still hoped-for unity of eu-

---

[2] "Together at the Lord's Table". EKD Council underlines statement of the Ecumenical Working Group, EKD press release of 28.02.2020, https://www.ekd.de/gemeinsam-am-tisch-des-herrn-53611.htm.

charistic fellowship. As we work together in ecumenism, we do not have to concentrate on this one goal alone, but it is the life blood of ecumenism and thus a goal which we indeed cannot simply put into practice, but which we should keep firmly in view in all our ecumenical efforts. To this end, this booklet of materials forms another building block, and I hope it will be widely used, particularly in the preparation of the Assembly and in liturgical practice.

Hanover, May 2022

Bishop Petra Bosse-Huber

2.3 Council of Churches in Germany (Archpriest Radu Constantin Miron)

Almost 20 years ago, in 2003, the member churches of the Council of Churches in Germany (ACK) committed themselves in the Charta Oecumenica to "move towards the goal of eucharistic fellowship", characterising the lack of eucharistic fellowship as "a particularly painful sign of the divisions among many Christian churches" (ChOe 5). We as ACK continue to feel committed to this mission.

Nonetheless, we are also well aware of the difficulties that lie ahead. Among other things, the theological discussion concerns questions of the respective understanding of ministry, the prerequisites for eucharistic fellowship and the understanding of the respective celebration. We are particularly confronted with such differences of understanding and tradition in the ACK.

At the same time, we perceive that more and more people fail to understand why eucharistic fellowship cannot take place. This applies first of all to people who have a reserved attitude towards the Church, but it is now increasingly true of those who are active and close to the Church and are frustrated by the apparent lack of progress on this issue. The consequence of such a lack of understanding is often indifference towards theological and denominational positions, and that usually leads to decisions made on a personal and individual basis.

In this context, married couples and families of mixed denominations are placed in a very special dilemma, since they are daily confronted with this rift in Christian fellowship. We face the ecumenical challenge of ensuring that they do not break down under this tension, but find mutual ways to live out and pass on their Christian faith in a convincing way.

In the midst of this complicated mixture of resignation, determination and indifference, two documents on the topic of Eucharist/Holy Communion have emerged from multilateral ecumenical contexts.

First of all, I congratulate the editors of this publication for pursuing the goal of taking up the encouraging impulses from the 3rd Ecumenical Kirchentag, which was held digitally and decentrally due to the pandemic, passing them on and making them fruitful on an international level. Getting to know the different traditions that celebrate the memory of Jesus Christ can be a first step towards ecumenical understanding and can also lead to more intensive contact and exchange between the Christian communities, true to the theological motto "lex orandi – lex credendi". I can observe that this is already happening in many places at the local level and that it is a good thing if we now follow this impulse at higher levels and in wider regions.

The German Ecumenical Study Committee (DÖSTA) of the ACK has also considered the topic of "Eucharist, Holy Communion, Holy Sacrifice" in various formats over a period of several years. One result of this process is to be found in this booklet: the joint statement of the DÖSTA. In addition, the DÖSTA has pursued the goal of compiling a synopsis of the forms of celebration of the member churches of the ACK in order to improve their mutual understanding. These findings were deepened at a conference in which they were respectively presented by a member of a different denomination (in the sense of external representation). All these results have been published in an ACK documentation: *Miteinander beten, singen und Gottesdienst feiern."*

Together, these two publications can strengthen the ecumenical will to restart the discussion on how the presence of Jesus Christ is celebrated, jointly seeking ways to overcome this particularly painful sign of our divisions, the lack of eucharistic fellowship.

Thus we as the Council of Churches in Germany are grateful that this issue will also be a topic at the 11th Assembly of the World Council of Churches in Karlsruhe on 5 September 2022. It shows that the yearning is still strong, and that the churches in Germany are not prepared to accept passively the scandal of separation, but are working together to become more and more united as a community. This is what we are doing in the ACK, strengthened by the Charta Oecumenica and by the Assembly's pledge: "The love of Christ moves, reconciles and unites the world."

Archpriest Radu Constantin Miron

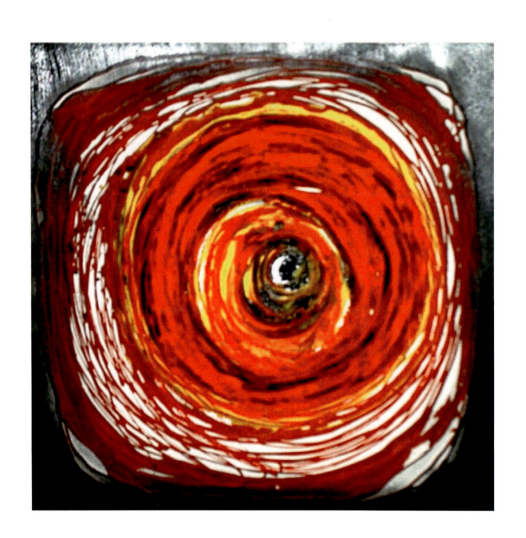

3 Ecumenical theological insights

(Hacik Gazer, Markus Iff, Werner Klän and Dorothea Sattler)

3.1 Spiritual ecumenism in the context of other approaches to ecumenism

Spiritual ecumenism is extremely important for the future of the churches. After fruitful decades of understanding on theological issues, the ecumenical movement now faces new challenges: fundamental questions of faith, in which the churches have common options, are introduced into the social discussions. As the large churches are losing their significance, it seems more important than ever *today* to address the challenges of world politics, social and personal ethics together.

All churches are challenged to face the pressing present-day questions. How can people find a safe place to live their lives? How is it possible to achieve reconciliation and peace among the nations? How can the basic necessities of life be secured for all? Why is it not possible to distribute paid employment fairly? Who can satisfy the hunger and thirst of the needy in countries where it rarely rains? In what way can the complications be resolved that many people feel with regard to their lives in relationships? Who can stand day and night alongside people in despair? Who will comfort the dying with the Easter message of our common Christian gospel?

In ecumenical encounters, true spiritual experiences leave much to be desired – in a positive sense: when they take place, the grief at the ongoing separation can be strongly felt, and at the same time they convey a gratifying sense of the great richness of the Christian faith. What remains is the desire for a lively Christian fellowship which is not threatened by separation, but marked by attentiveness to God's Word, sacramental remembrance of the death and resurrection of Jesus Christ, praise and worship of the Triune God and willingness to witness in word and deed.

Through spiritual experiences, people are consciously led by the power of the presence of the Spirit of God to the depths of their existential questions, and they sense that they can recognise and accept trustworthy answers. But it can only be a move in the direction of the divine mystery: "For we know only in part, and we prophesy only in part; but when the complete comes, the partial will come to an end." (1 Cor 13:9f.)

This spiritual journey of the Christian confessions can take a variety of outward forms according to the respective situation and tradition: silent listening, urgent pleading, persistent singing, courageous action, symbolic gestures, open conversations. Anyone who has ever experienced that other people can express in a plausible and appealing way the answers they themselves have found in the common questions of life will no longer want to forego the attraction of spiritual togetherness. Life leaves much to be desired. In companionship, it is easier to enter into the darknesses of existence, to consider the unavoidability of death and the burden of sin. It is only in fellowship that one can protect the light of trust in the God of life.

Spiritual ecumenism can be considered as a guiding concept governing the social and missionary aspects of ecumenism. Christians are living and acting spiritually if they allow themselves to be touched by the encounter with the poorest of the poor, whether materially or spiritually. The gospel is not merely proclaimed in the one form, as a spoken word; when we serve one another wordlessly, we are also witnesses as Christ's followers. Ecumenical conversations have an important significance of their own: in dialogues we promise one another that we will be attentive to the way of life of people of other denominations. Conversations do not only function on the objective level, they also create existential relationships.

3.2 The common confession of Jesus Christ as the basis of ecumenical action

At the end of his earthly life, Jesus Christ prays to God for the unity of the people who confess him: "May all be one. As you, Father, are in me and I am in you, may they also be in us, so that the world may believe that you have sent me" (John 17:21). There is a connection between the credibility of the Christian confession and the way people live in fellowship, reconciled with one another as followers of Jesus. There is no alternative to the task of achieving ecumenical conviction among all Christian traditions, given Jesus' request, handed down in biblical tradition, that the disciples be united in following him. Discipleship of Jesus Christ means to live humbly, peaceably and patiently with one another (cf. Ephesians 4:2). It is the one faith in Christ, the one baptism and the one Trinitarian confession of God which unites the Christian confessions across all boundaries of time and space in the *oikumene*, the one world inhabited by God's creatures.

Effective remembrance of Jesus Christ is the mission of ecumenism. Jesus experiences his deep connection with God as calling and empowerment to love the people he meets. Those who are sick, forgotten and despised experience his – and at the same time God's – healing attention. So is God: he lives as a human being among humans, so that they can recognise him by his love. Ecumenism, the remembrance of Christ in God's Spirit, therefore has a profoundly diaconal dimension. Christians trust that all human efforts to preserve creation are inspired and supported by God's Spirit. Ethics based on creation theology, the cry for justice for all living beings, concern for the preservation of the conditions of life, resistance against all forms of violence that are hostile to humanity – these things are central to the mission of ecumenism.

It is not by chance that early ecumenical relationships which have proven stable and effective are to be found in the area of so-called "categorial pastoral care". Unlike in the local churches, where people live permanently with their families, it deals with people who are only affected temporarily. The concern of pastoral care is to proclaim Christian hope particularly to people in critical phases of life: for example, in telephone counselling, hospice work, railway mission or also in military chaplaincy. Being charitable and giving hope is the mission of all Christian churches. Liturgy, diakonia and proclamation are closely linked as the three basic dimensions of church action. The liturgical celebration of the Holy Communion and the Eucharist is a witness to God's action in Jesus Christ. God's Spirit reminds us actively of Jesus Christ and enables us to follow him in word and deed. The gospel needs to be lived and witnessed today in ecumenical solidarity.

3.3 Convergences achieved in the area of Holy Communion, Eucharist and Holy Sacrifice

For many decades, the churches have held ecumenical conversations at various levels (local, regional, national and worldwide), primarily regarding topics that were highly relevant in the context of historical controversies. Many points of agreement have been reached in individual areas of the doctrine of the Holy Communion, Eucharist and Holy Sacrifice.

3.3.1 Holy Communion and Eucharist – a "sacrifice"?

Against the backdrop of the controversies in the 16th century, one of the issues charged to ecumenism is the understanding of the Holy Communion and the Eucharist as "sacrifice". All Christian traditions subscribe to this interpretation of Jesus' loving gift of his own life to the utmost, even to his own death, especially according to the theology of the Letter to the Hebrews. A misleading use of the term "sacrifice" is given when the impression arises that God demanded Jesus' death in order to reconcile himself with creation. It is not the people, not the churches, who offer a sacrifice to God. In truth, the movement goes in a very different direction: God gives us the testimony of his Son's life in order to bear ultimate witness to his readiness to reconcile. In the liturgy this is made clear in the anaphora, the eucharistic prayer.

Basic agreements were reached in ecumenical studies: the death of Jesus Christ, his loving gift of his life, is made present as the congregation celebrates the Lord's Supper as a sacrament and a means of blessing. In the Holy Communion and the Eucharist, the congregation celebrates the memory of Jesus' life by the working of the Holy Spirit – right down to his last gift, his death for us. The confession of the uniqueness and singularity of Jesus Christ's gift of himself in his life and death forms the basis of all considerations regarding the sacrificial character of the Holy Communion and the Eucharist.

Through the liturgical actions and the communion of believers and baptised in the celebration of the Holy Communion and Eucharist, the meaning of Jesus' life and death for us is effectively remembered. In the words of interpretation, in the breaking of the bread in which Christ himself becomes nourishment for us, and in the one shared cup of Christ's blood from which all drink, the reconciliation promised by God to all sinners is celebrated. The congregation joins in the sacrifice of praise and thanksgiving for God's action towards us. All who celebrate the gift of redemption are subsequently called to act themselves as a human sign of God's mercy and also to spend their lives following Jesus in the service of reconciliation.

3.3.2 True presence of Jesus Christ in the meal (Real Presence)

When it came to the theological understanding of the Holy Communion, the disputes between the Lutheran and Reformed traditions in the 16th century were more serious than those between the Old Believers (Roman Catholics) and the Lutherans. The two Reformation groups quarrelled in particular over the question whether the presence of Jesus Christ in the meal was (also) bodily (Lutheran view) or (solely) spiritual (Reformed view). The Roman Catholic side was critically questioned as to whether the favoured doctrine of transubstantiation was not based more on philosophy than theology.

In ecumenical studies of the three models of the eucharistic Real Presence competing in the 16th century (Roman Catholic, Lutheran and Reformed), it became clear that from today's perspective they are considered compatible against the background of the respective guiding theological interests. Together, the confessions recognise the pneumatological orientation, the appeal to the action of God's Spirit, in Reformed eucharistic theology; together, the Lutheran and Roman Catholic traditions recognise that the controversies surrounding the concept of substance can be ignored from today's perspective, because they were formulated in the 16th century under presuppositions that no longer apply today. Together, all confessional traditions are aware that the eucharistic mystery is described by human thoughts that cannot do full justice to divine reality. Against the background of this basic insight, three confessional approaches to understanding the presence of Jesus Christ in the Holy Communion and the Eucharist can be held in esteem jointly:

(1) The Roman Catholic doctrine of transubstantiation assumes a transformation of the essence of the gifts at the meal (substantia), while retaining their outward manifestations (accidentia); this model, developed in the 13th century by Thomas Aquinas, seeks to avoid the dilemma both of realism (people eat Jesus) and symbolism (the symbolic action merely refers

to a past event); the historical achievement of the doctrine of transubstantiation is widely recognised ecumenically today.

(2) The Lutheran tradition rejects the human claim to be able to describe the eucharistic mystery adequately with philosophical categories (accusation of sophistry). In the debates of the 16th century, none of those involved understood the medieval concept of substance (based on Aristotle), which does not pay attention to the material, but rather primarily focuses on the purpose, the meaning, the essence of a being. The Lutheran reference to the "real presence of the body and blood of Christ in the sacrament of the altar" means that Christ distributes in Holy Communion what he has instituted, in order to redeem the world. In doing so, it does not in the least deny an equally real – i.e. personal – presence of the Lord of the Church, which it also recognises in other liturgies of the Word and of prayer. However, it strives to determine the way in which Christ is specially present in the sacrament of the altar. This kind of (real) presence of the "body and blood of Christ" is based on Christ's words in the power of creation and is considered to be without analogy.

(3) The Reformed tradition has difficulty with the idea that the resurrected and exalted Jesus Christ can be present again in his human nature in the celebration of the Eucharist. The Reformed tradition teaches a real presence of Jesus Christ in the form of his presence in the Holy Spirit; thus it "loosens" the reference to the gifts of the meal and faces the question of whether human consciousness (believing or unbelieving) is the decisive criterion for the realisation of the real presence of Jesus Christ. To put it simply: do unbelievers (just) eat bread, while believers (alone) experience true communion with Jesus Christ?

In current ecumenical conversations, the three positions described above are respected as human ways of describing the one mystery of the presence of Jesus Christ. In each case, two of the three concepts share a common concern:

(1) Lutherans and Reformed oppose the doctrine of transubstantiation because it (supposedly) gives the impression that humans can explain the mystery of the divine presence with the aid of philosophical categories.

(2) Lutherans and Roman Catholics oppose the Reformed because in this concept human consciousness (moved by God's Spirit) is apparently decisive for the presence of Jesus Christ.

(3) Reformed and Roman Catholics oppose the Lutherans because the idea that Christ is omnipresent in his human nature hardly makes it possible to express the specific way in which Christ is present in Holy Communion, Eucharist and Holy Sacrifice by the power of the Spirit of God.

Together, all three traditions today advocate a real-symbolic understanding of the presence of Jesus Christ, in which the original purpose of the eucharistic meal as it was instituted plays the most important role: Jesus himself broke a loaf and shared a cup of wine. Jesus declared that these gestures of offering symbolised the willing gift of his life for us. With his life, Jesus Christ testifies that God wants sinners to live and not to die. Participation in the eucharistic event also (lastingly) transforms the communion of those celebrating and calls them to follow Jesus Christ. All this happens in the power of God's Spirit.

The Protestant free churches and associations, such as the Methodist Church, the Baptists, the Mennonites, the Evangelical Free Churches and the Pentecostal churches,[1] which are part of the global network of Protestantism, are also mostly in agreement with a real-symbolic understanding of the presence of Jesus Christ, based on the original purpose of Jesus' meal with his disciples, when he broke the bread and passed the cup.

They focus on the celebration of the Holy Communion as a whole and not exclusively on the words of institution *(verba testamenti)*; they do not pay strict attention to an interpretation of the gifts based on the words spoken over them. Even where Protestant free churches avoid the definition sacrament with regard to the Holy Communion and the Eucharist, they do indeed reckon with God's blessed work of grace at the communion service, so that spiritually they cultivate a sacramental understanding.[2]

---

[1] Ulrich Körtner, Ökumenische Kirchenkunde. Lehrwerk Evangelische Theologie (LETh) 9, Leipzig 2018. Vereinigung Evangelischer Freikirchen (ed.), Freikirchenhandbuch. Information-Texte-Berichte, Wuppertal 2004.

[2] Cf., among others, Jean-Daniel Plüss, Sacrament or Ordinance: A Pentecostal Approach to a Contentious Issue in Corneliu Constantineanu and Christopher J. Scobie eds. Pentecostals in the 21st Century: Identity, Belief, Praxis, Eugene, OR, Wipf and Stock Publishers, 2018, 59-74.

Concordia-Lutheran churches, in accordance with the Lutheran confessions of the 16th century, and in the certainty that they are speaking according to the text of Scripture, firmly uphold the true presence of the body and blood of Christ in the altar sacrament and in the distribution of these gifts and their effect to those who receive the sacrament. Thus, in the celebration of the sacrament, the identity of bread and wine with the body and blood of Christ is truly accomplished through the creative power of Jesus' words of institution. The "consecration" of the eucharistic gifts of bread and wine occurs within an overall process of worship. This includes the assembly at the service of worship, the preparation of the gifts, their blessing by the Lord's words of institution, the distribution, the reception, the eating and drinking, and the proclamation of the salvation achieved by Christ through the gift of himself.

3.4 Connecting the meaning with the form of the liturgy

3.4.1 Liturgical reforms are now made in the ecumenical context

At the very beginning of the first document published by the Second Vatican Council (1962-65), the Liturgical Constitution "Sacrosanctum Concilium" (SC), one can discern a great ecumenical breadth when it states that the reform of the liturgy sought by the Council desires "to foster whatever can promote union among all who believe in Christ" (SC 1). The same intention is to be found in the *Evangelisches Gottesdienstbuch* (Protestant Book of Worship), first published in 2000 and in 2020 in a second edition. Here it says: "The Protestant worship service is lively related to the services of the other churches in ecumenism."[3]

The Greek Orthodox theologian Grigorios Larentzakis writes: "In all phases of their lives, all Christians are spiritually accompanied as a community that praises God, prays and worships – a community in which each and every one can develop their ministries and charisms in order to grow in perfection and achieve communion with the Triune God."[4]

---

[3] Evangelisches Gottesdienstbuch. Agende für die Evangelische Kirche der Union und für die Vereinigte Evangelisch-Lutherische Kirche Deutschlands, Bielefeld/ Leipzig 2020, 17.

[4] Larentzakis, Grigorios: Die orthodoxe Kirche. Ihr Leben und ihr Glaube, in: orientalia – patristica – oecumenica, Vol. 4, ed. Dietmar W. Winkler, LIT Verlag GmbH &

3.4.2 The meaning of the Holy Communion and the Eucharist is the celebration of the paschal mystery

The Second Vatican Council replies to the central question of what we celebrate in the liturgy of the Church by saying that this is always a celebration of the paschal mystery of Jesus Christ. The Council explains the term "Paschal Mystery" more precisely in the Constitution on the Liturgy, where it says: "The wonderful works of God ... were but a prelude to the work of Christ the Lord in redeeming mankind .... He achieved His task principally by the paschal mystery of His blessed passion, resurrection from the dead, and the glorious ascension" (SC 5). The Council re-establishes the breadth of salvation history. Every liturgical celebration is related to the paschal mystery. This can be experienced in a particularly intense and compact way in the celebration of the Holy Communion, the Eucharist, which is therefore characterised by the Second Vatican Council as the "fount and apex" of the whole Christian life (cf. Dogmatic Constitution "Lumen Gentium", 11).

In the Protestant Book of Worship, the two basic forms of service of the word can be combined with the celebration of Holy Communion. The heart of the Protestant service is the gathering of the congregation to hear God's word, to call upon God in the face of hardship in life, and to give thanks to him for all the good he has given.

The Protestant free churches, too, see the meaning of the Holy Communion, in accordance with the biblical traditions, in the fact that Jesus Christ, the crucified, raised and exalted Lord, unites the participants in the meal with himself and with each other in the fellowship of his body, builds his church and strengthens the believers. They emphasise in particular that the congregation gathered in the name of Jesus Christ, as a believing community of his followers, is constitutive for carrying out the meal as a gift of God and an act of thanksgiving by those who receive it.

According to the (Concordia-)Lutheran view, the celebration of the holy meal is always a celebration by the church of Jesus Christ; the sacrament is central to the people of God. The "consecration" of the eucharistic

---

Co. KG, Wien 32012, 166.

gifts of bread and wine is part of a comprehensive liturgical celebration. This includes the assembly of the congregation at worship, the preparation of the gifts, their blessing by the Lord's words of institution, the distribution, reception, eating and drinking of these gifts, and the proclamation of the salvation achieved by Christ through the gift of himself.

"The sacraments," says Ecumenical Patriarch Bartholomew I, "offer another way of relating to God and the world, in which everything is received and shared as a gift of encounter and communion. [...] Communion is indispensable for sharing with one another. It is a powerful and privileged experience of encounter with God."[5]

3.4.3 The weekly rhythm

Since the time of the early church, the celebration of the Holy Communion was particularly related to the celebration of the Lord's Day, Sunday, the day commemorating the resurrection of Jesus Christ. Ecumenical convergence exists in the conviction that Sunday is to be sanctified.

The weekly rhythm in the celebration of the Christian liturgy is to be understood as an adoption of the Jewish Sabbath tradition. At the same time, when Christian communities began to be formed, it was evidently the practice to gather daily to combine the remembrance of Jesus with a meal (cf. Acts 2:46). Social differences (cf. 1 Corinthians 11:17-22) were probably the reason why Christians very soon made a distinction between the daily meal to satisfy hunger and the ritualised form commemorating the life, death and resurrection of Jesus Christ instituted by him with the two features: breaking the bread and sharing the cup. As the eucharistic liturgy became increasingly detached from the nourishing meal, the weekly rhythm prevailed.

In the Western Latin tradition – partly in connection with the increasing focus on the commemoration of the dead – the idea of the daily Eucharist took predominance. In the Reformation tradition, the weekly rhythm was preserved with regard to the liturgy of the Word of God; at the same time, the question of worthy or unworthy participation in the Holy Communion (cf. 1 Corinthians 11:27) came into the forefront: only those who knew

---

[5] Ecumenical Patriarch Bartholomew I: Begegnung mit dem Mysterium. Das orthodoxe Christentum von heute verstehen, Verlag Ferdinand Schöningh, Paderborn 2019, 69.

themselves to be free from sin should take part at Communion. As a consequence, a distinction was made between the gathering of the whole congregation to hold the service of the Word of God, and the celebration of Holy Communion by a smaller number who had prepared themselves accordingly through repentance and confession of sin. If Holy Communion is celebrated less frequently in the Protestant tradition, it should thus be understood as an expression of the special esteem in which this liturgy is held – and not that it is less highly regarded. This also applies to the Protestant free churches. In the context of the German Protestant Kirchentag movement, aspects of communion piety have once again come to the fore which place a stronger emphasis on the joy of the meal, the gifts of creation given by God, the glad fellowship with Jesus. It is one concern of the Protestant Kirchentag to focus more on the need in the world in a political context, rather than on individual need in view of one's own sin, by organising a "celebration supper".

Today, all Christian traditions are challenged to reflect on their experiences with regard to the rhythm of church services. New forms are emerging that concentrate not so much on fixed schedules, but rather on situations and occasions. The Roman Catholic liturgical reform at the Second Vatican Council also made it clear that the liturgy of the Word of God is of great importance in this respect (cf. SC 35). Patriarch Bartholomew writes: "Prayer presupposes a life that is integrated into the life of the world and is not something that takes place at a certain point in our daily or weekly routine. Our goal of reciting prayers on given occasions and withdrawing to pray at certain moments means that we should move on from the stage of saying the prayers, and become prayer ourselves."[6]

3.4.4 The aim is active participation of all in the liturgies

The denominations are nowadays united in their concern to let the entire congregation participate in the liturgies. The Reformation tradition played a major role when the Second Vatican Council ensured that the Roman Catholic liturgies were held all over the world in a language that could be understood by the worshippers. In the liturgical celebration of the Eucharist, those attending the service celebrating should by no means be

---

[6] Ibid, 64.

"strangers and silent spectators" (cf. SC 48), but according to the will of the Council and the intention of the most recent liturgical reform, they should participate fully consciously and actively in the celebration of the liturgy (cf. SC 14), meaning that they should (be able to) actively understand and celebrate it inwardly and outwardly. Protestant free churches understand and plan the Holy Communion as a dynamic event marking the presence of Jesus Christ, remembrance and thanksgiving of the congregation. Therefore, they attach importance to the participation of the whole congregation in thanksgiving, epiclesis and anamnesis.

According to the (Concordia-)Lutheran confessions, the church as the body of Christ is the "bearer of church authority". What is given to the whole church comes into practice in the local congregation. For the Christian congregation – irrespective of the manifold forms in which it may appear – is the place *where* and *in which* everything takes place that Jesus Christ has commissioned his Christianity to do. The ministry of the church is therefore not *above* but *within* the congregation. In all cases the interrelation between ministry and congregation is indissoluble.

Orthodox liturgies, on the other hand, often give the impression that the faithful are apathetic observers, because they do not join in the singing. Larentzakis says: "First of all, it must be said that the Divine Liturgy actually takes the form of a dialogue between the liturgists and the 'people'. However, the development and refinement of church music meant that in many churches the people are not able to join in singing this music. The people have been replaced by the choir. Nevertheless, the participation in the Divine Liturgy and the spiritual experience in the celebration of the Mystery in the eucharistic assembly is not the same as it is understood and practised in the West. Inner participation can also take place in the church by keeping silent and listening. The intensity of emotional experience is not necessarily dependent on active participation. With this, I also want to point to another aspect and another experience of Orthodox spirituality which is not fully appreciated everywhere."[7]

---

[7] Larentzakis, Die Orthodoxe Kirche (see footnote 10), 171.

3.4.5 The experience of church communion is effected by the Holy Spirit

The celebration of the Holy Communion and the Eucharist not only presupposes church communion, but at the same time creates it through the spiritual conversion of the congregation gathered for the Lord's Supper, directed towards the unifying centre in faith in Jesus Christ. According to common ecumenical conviction, it is God's Spirit that promotes unity. This central aspect of the epicletic prayer within the celebration of the Holy Communion and Eucharist has to be taken into account when it comes to the ecumenically sensitive form of denominational services. For example, one prayer in the Protestant Book of Worship reads: "In this meal, let us all become one body in Jesus Christ."[8] In the second Eucharistic Prayer according to the Roman Catholic order, the congregation prays that "we may be gathered into one by the Holy Spirit."[9] The Third Eucharistic Prayer says: "Grant that we, who are nourished by the Body and Blood of your Son and filled with his Holy Spirit, may become one body, one spirit in Christ.".[10]

In the Orthodox liturgy, too, the church communion is manifested in the bread and wine. "In the Cherubimic Hymn before the Great Entrance, when the gifts of wine and bread are brought to the altar, it says 'Let us, who mystically represent the Cherubim and chant the thrice-holy hymn to the life-creating Trinity, now lay aside all earthly cares, that we may receive the King of all, who comes invisibly upborne in triumph by the ranks of angels.' No one remains unmoved by this moment of the Great Entrance as the procession moves through the nave of the church where the believers are standing. Some of them bow while crossing themselves, some prostrate themselves, others fall down as the procession passes, imploring mercy and help from their King and Saviour, even though the gifts being carried have not yet been transformed into the precious body and blood of the Lord. Here, it is not only evident that the images of the earthly liturgy

---

[8] Evangelisches Gottesdienstbuch (see footnote 9), 80.
[9] The Roman Missal 2010, International Commission on English in the Liturgy Corporation (ICEL)
[10] Ibid.

are a reflection of the heavenly liturgy, but also that the two are connected to each other, because the faithful 'mystically represent the cherubim'."[11]

3.4.6 Unity in legitimate diversity is to be shaped

Every denominational liturgical form for the celebration of the Lord's Supper, Eucharist and Holy Sacrifice lives on its tradition, but is at the same time open towards specific situations in which the service takes place. Despite the commitment to a basic sequence of a Roman Catholic celebration of the Mass, the concrete format of this liturgy permits a sensitive understanding for the people gathered here to celebrate the Eucharist. Taking up concerns of the Second Vatican Council (cf. SC 14; 37-40), Pope Francis repeatedly emphasises the outstanding importance of the participation of the entire congregation in worship, as well as the need to shape the liturgy according to the local culture. The Protestant Book of Worship also emphasises the connection "with the particular history and characterisic of each congregation."[12] The language of the liturgy is especially important in this regard. Thus, the Protestant Book of Worship states: "No one should be excluded by the language."[13] The Orthodox tradition also agrees with the basic idea that diversity of liturgies is legitimate, corresponding to specific occasions. "Spiritual guidance is given by liturgical life. There are separate prayers for the various occasions in the life of Christians, spoken by the priest or bishop. To mention only a few: there are prayers for sick people and animals, for the laying of the foundation stone of a house or its first occupancy, for the digging of a water well, for the fields, gardens, vineyards and their protection against natural disasters; for the blessing of fruit, grain, wine or a herd of animals, for the building of a ship, for the blessing of the nets, for the blessing of bread, meat, cheese and eggs; prayers for travellers, for favourable winds and the prevention of storms at sea. Recently, at the instigation of the Ecumenical Patriarchate, all Orthodox Churches have accepted that September 1 each year be liturgically designated for creation and the environment. There are also special liturgical acts for particular occasions, such as the beginning of the school year, the inauguration of a private business or a social institution, for the laying

---

[11] Larentzakis, Die Orthodoxe Kirche, 171.
[12] Evangelisches Gottesdienstbuch, 20
[13] Ibid., 18

of the foundation stone of a church, a school or some other building; for the opening of a charitable institution, a new irrigation system, a new ship, a new vehicle or the founding of a new public authority. Other acts are a doxology (Te Deum) after a city has been rescued from enemies, a memorial service for those killed in war, the New Year's blessing on January 1, or the blessing on the 1st of each month by the liturgy of the consecration of water. (...) The centre and foundation of all these liturgical acts is the Divine Liturgy, the Holy Eucharist. The variety of these liturgical acts with their special texts do not only reveal a beautiful hymnological treasure with remarkable content, but also testify to the deep concern of the Orthodox Church and its care for all spheres of human existence. This means not only spiritual accompaniment, but also support, help, encouragement, restoration, loving solidarity and solace. And this is exactly what also happens within the Holy Eucharist, within the Divine Liturgy, but in an even more compressed form, although we are sadly often not conscious of it."[14]

3.5 Church communion and communion at the eucharistic meal

Official church statements currently demonstrate different approaches when it comes to determining the prerequisites for practising fellowship at the celebration of the Holy Communion and the Eucharist. The point of difference here lies in the question of the extent to which an already existing communion of churches is the prerequisite for eucharistic communion.

The Orthodox tradition tends to apply the strictest criteria regarding the communion of belief and church as a prerequisite for eucharistic fellowship. Since the Orthodox churches do not appear to be able even to recognise baptism performed in the Western churches, there is no need for further considerations in this respect. By signing the Magdeburg Declaration on the mutual recognition of baptism, the expatriate Orthodox communities in Germany have gone their own way.

The doctrinal texts of the Western churches also advocate a close connection between church communion and eucharistic communion. At the same time, the Roman Catholic tradition describes exceptions in which

---
[14] Larentzakis, Die Orthodoxe Kirche, 168f.

participation in the celebration is possible for reasons of pastoral concern. Here the principle applies that, with regard to the aim of the ecumenical movement, the unity of the church(es) must also be respected within institutions; on the other hand, the grace to be had from common worship for individual believers in Christ and their families "sometimes commends this practice".[15]

Accordingly, exceptions are foreseen. The connection between communion of faith and Holy Communion is not unknown to the Protestant tradition in German regional churches, but here there is a different emphasis. If there is a common understanding of the Lord's Supper, all believers in Christ are invited to the celebration. Jesus Christ himself extends this invitation in the Holy Spirit. On the basis of the recognition that the remaining differences are not sufficient to divide the church, the Leuenberg Agreement (1973) states that table and pulpit fellowship exists in future between the Reformation churches. From the outset it was agreed that further discussions should deepen the common theological positions. In consistency with the mutual recognition of baptism (Magdeburg Declaration of 2007), (Concordia-)Lutherans can express recognition that the other church signatories are real churches. This also concerns the dimension of "spiritual ecumenism", which is a noteworthy reality lying below the threshold of declared church communion. The Independent Evangelical Lutheran Church (SELK) also recognises a "pastorally responsible eucharistic hospitality", although it distinguishes this categorially from church communion in word and sacrament and the practice of the "open altar". Such hospitality is not excluded, despite the theological differences that have been identified. However, it presupposes – at least on the part of the SELK and its pastors – an examination of each individual case.

---

[15] Second Vatican Council, Decree "Unitatis Redintegratio", 8,4.

4 Exemplary selected ecumenical dialogues

(Hacik Gazer, Markus Iff, Werner Klän and Dorothea Sattler)

In the ecumenical movement, there are different opinions as to the importance of theological conversations in the search for the unity of the churches. With regard to dialogue ecumenism, the pros and cons have often been considered critically and questions formulated. What is the real-life relevance of the topics discussed in the committees? Are they not mostly dealing with controversial theological aspects whose origins lie way back in the past and whose relevance can hardly be recognised when the congregations hold their services? Is it not so, that liturgical traditions have developed in the various Christian denominations without being reflected intellectually? What realistic goals are attainable?

Here, in multilateral collegial ecumenical fellowship, we speak up for the enduring importance of theological reflection in ecumenical conversations for the following reasons. Each in their own ways, people in the churches seek to preserve the memory of Jesus Christ. They are enriched when exchanging their views in conversation about what is considered essential in individual traditions. It is not necessarily the purpose of the dialogues to convince others of one's own point of view or to persuade them to change their behaviour. Information about other denominations, especially about observations that appear strange to one's own, can be thought-provoking and a motivation to self-critical examination of one's own position. When a liturgical celebration emphasises different aspects of meaning, one may be inclined to pay closer attention. Misunderstandings can be recognised as such. Commonalities that are noticed in the proclamation of the Christian gospel reinforce faith. If the dialogues are conducted in a spirit of enquiry, they will reveal the difference between the manifold attempts made by humans over many centuries to grasp the mystery of God's action intellectually, and the common trust in the efficacy of the promise he has given.

On the subject of the Eucharist, Holy Communion and Holy Sacrifice, individual conversations have been held again and again between many denominations in recent decades.[1] Of outstanding importance in multilateral ecumenism to this day are the Lima Declarations of Convergence of the Faith and Order Commission of 1982, which, in addition to baptism and ministry, also cover the subject of the Eucharist. It is well worth re-reading this text, which is reproduced here in full (section 4.1) in order to focus on the understanding already reached in the multilateral context as well as on the questions which are still open. From our point of view, it would be very desirable if, after the long period of dialogues that have been conducted in the meantime, the discussion on this topic could be conducted anew multilaterally with church delegations at the global level. A beginning has been made on a national multilateral level with the document of the German Ecumenical Study Committee (chapter 5 in this book). In addition, individual results of bilateral dialogues are presented here, which can demonstrate that individual denominations are each engaged in discussions on what they see as relevant (controversial) issues (section 4.2). In Europe, the "Leuenberg Agreement" (1973) agreed between the Lutheran and Reformed churches is of very high significance in terms of practical effect (section 4.3). The bilateral study "Together at the Lord's Table" by the Ecumenical Working Group of Protestant and Catholic Theologians, which has been widely discussed not only in the German-speaking world, is presented here separately (section 4.4), because it makes a plea for specific action, which is distinct from a mere ecumenical exchange of theological insights.

4.1 Multilateral: Declaration of Convergence on the topic of "Eucharist" (Faith and Order, Lima 1982)

The first conference of the "Faith and Order Movement" (Faith and Order) was in Lausanne in 1927. Since the founding of the World Council

---

[1] Cf. as intrroduction with many bibliographic notes: Susan Wood, Die Eucharistie: Ökumenische Errungenschaften und bleibende Unterschiede, in: Ökumenische Rundschau 61 (2012), 389-410.

of Churches in Amsterdam in 1948, this fountainhead of the ecumenical movement has introduced discussions on theological issues related to Christian faith and the institutional life of the churches. Whilst at the outset the various Reformation and Orthodox theologies were brought into dialogue with one another, the situation changed in 1968 after the Second Vatican Council when the Roman Catholic Church joined Faith and Order. Thus, the text of 1982 quoted here formulated with Roman Catholic participation. The Lima Convergence Declaration was preceded by preliminary studies in which the Anglican Communion of Churches was particularly intensively involved. Unlike any other ecumenical dialogue event, the Lima Convergence Declarations have to a high degree experienced a worldwide reception by responsible church officials, which has also been published.[2] The excerpt from the overall document of the Lima Convergence Declaration presented here on the topic of "Eucharist" makes reference to the other topics of "Baptism" and "Ministry," since from the perspective of many denominations baptism is the prerequisite for participation in the Eucharist, and ordination is expected as a condition for the ministry of leading the celebration of the Eucharist.

Eucharist

I. The Institution of the Eucharist

1. The Church receives the eucharist as a gift from the Lord. St Paul wrote: "I have received from the Lord what I also delivered to you, that the Lord Jesus on the night when he was betrayed took bread, and when he had given thanks, he broke it, and said: 'This is my body, which is for you. Do this in remembrance (anamnesis) of me.' In the same way also the cup, after supper, saying: 'This cup is the new covenant in my blood. Do this, as often as you drink it, in remembrance of me.' " (I Cor. 11:23–25; cf. Matt. 26:26–29; Mark 14:22–25; Luke 22:14–20).

The meals which Jesus is recorded as sharing during his earthly ministry proclaim and enact the nearness of the Kingdom, of which the feeding of the multitudes is a sign. In his last meal, the fellowship of the Kingdom was connected with the imminence of Jesus' suffering. After his resurrec-

---

[2] Cf. Max Thurian (ed.), Churches Respond to BEM [Baptism, Eucharist, Ministry], 6 Vols., Geneva 1986-1988. A summary can be found in: Baptism, Eucharist & Ministry 1982-1990. Report on the Process and Responses, WCC, 1990, 160pp.

tion, the Lord made his presence known to his disciples in the breaking of the bread. Thus the eucharist continues these meals of Jesus during his earthly life and after his resurrection, always as a sign of the Kingdom. Christians see the eucharist prefigured in the Passover memorial of Israel's deliverance from the land of bondage and in the meal of the Covenant on Mount Sinai (Ex. 24). It is the new paschal meal of the Church, the meal of the New Covenant, which Christ gave to his disciples as the anamnesis of his death and resurrection, as the anticipation of the Supper of the Lamb (Rev. 19:9). Christ commanded his disciples thus to remember and encounter him in this sacramental meal, as the continuing people of God, until his return. The last meal celebrated by Jesus was a liturgical meal employing symbolic words and actions. Consequently the eucharist is a sacramental meal which by visible signs communicates to us God's love in Jesus Christ, the love by which Jesus loved his own "to the end" (John13:1). It has acquired many names: for example, the Lord's Supper, the breaking of bread, the holy communion, the divine liturgy, the mass. Its celebration continues as the central act of the Church's worship.

II The Meaning of the Eucharist

2. The Eucharist is above all the sacrament of the gift that God gives us in Christ through the power of the Holy Spirit. Every Christian receives this gift of salvation through communion in the body and blood of Christ. In the eucharistic meal, in the The eucharist is essentially the sacrament of the gift which God makes to us in Christ through the power of the Holy Spirit. Every Christian receives this gift of salvation through communion in the body and blood of Christ. In the eucharistic meal, in the eating and drinking of the bread and wine, Christ grants communion with himself. God himself acts, giving life to the body of Christ and renewing each member. In accordance with Christ's promise, each baptized member of the body of Christ receives in the eucharist the assurance of the forgiveness of sins (Matt. 26:28) and the pledge of eternal life (John 6:51-58). Although the eucharist is essentially one complete act, it will be considered here under the following aspects: thanksgiving to the Father, memorial of Christ, invocation of the Spirit, communion of the faithful, meal of the Kingdom.

A. The Eucharist as Thanksgiving to the Father

The eucharist, which always includes both word and sacrament, is a proclamation and a celebration of the work of God. It is the great thanksgiving to the Father for everything accomplished in creation, redemption and sanctification, for everything accomplished by God now in the Church and in the world in spite of the sins of human beings, for everything that God will accomplish in bringing the Kingdom to fulfilment. Thus the eucharist is the benediction (berakah) by which the Church expresses its thankfulness for all God's benefits.

1. The eucharist is the great sacrifice of praise by which the Church speaks on behalf of the whole creation. For the world which God has reconciled is pre- sent at every eucharist: in the bread and wine, in the persons of the faithful, and in the prayers they offer for themselves and for all people. Christ unites the faithful with himself and includes their prayers within his own intercession so that the faithful are trans- figured and their prayers accepted. This sacrifice of praise is possible only through Christ, with him and in him. The bread and wine, fruits of the earth and of human labour, are presented to the Father in faith and thanksgiving. The eucharist thus signifies what the world is to become: an offering and hymn of praise to the Creator, a universal communion in the body of Christ, a kingdom of justice, love and peace in the Holy Spirit.

B. The Eucharist as Anamnesis or Memorial of Christ

1. The eucharist is the memorial of the crucified and risen Christ, i.e. the living and effective sign of his sacrifice, accomplished once and for all on the cross and still operative on behalf of all humankind. The biblical idea of memorial as applied to the eucharist refers to this present efficacy of God's work when it is celebrated by God's people in a liturgy.

2. Christ himself with all that he has accomplished for us and for all creation (in his incarnation, servant-hood, ministry, teaching, suffering, sacrifice, resurrection, ascension and sending of the Spirit) is present in this anamnesis, granting us communion with himself. The eucharist is also the foretaste of his parousia and of the final kingdom.

3. The anamnesis in which Christ acts through the joyful celebration of his Church is thus both representation and anticipation. It is not only a calling to mind of what is past and of its significance. It is the Church's effective proclamation of God's mighty acts and promises.

4. Representation and _anticipation are expressed in thanksgiving and intercession. The Church, gratefully recalling God's mighty acts of redemption, beseeches God to give the benefits of these acts to every human being. In thanksgiving and intercession, the Church is united with the Son, its great High Priest and Intercessor (Rom. 8:34; Heb. 7:25). The eucharist is the sacrament of the unique sacrifice of Christ, who ever lives to make intercession for us. It is the memorial of all that God has done for the salvation of the world. What it was God's will to accomplish in the incarnation, life, death, resurrection and ascension of Christ, God does not repeat. These events are unique and can neither be repeated nor prolonged. In the memorial of the eucharist, however, the Church offers its intercession in communion with Christ, our great High Priest.

> *Commentary:*
>
> *It is in the light of the significance of the eucharist as intercession that references to the eucharist in Catholic theology as "propitiatory sacrifice" may be understood. The understanding is that there is only one expiation, that of the unique sacrifice of the cross, made actual in the eucharist and presented before the Father in the intercession of Christ and of the Church for all humanity.*
>
> *In the light of the biblical conception of memorial, all churches might want to review the old controversies about "sacrifice" and deepen their understanding of the reasons why other traditions than their own have either used or rejected this term.*

5. The anamnesis of Christ is the basis and source of all Christian prayer. So our prayer relies upon and is united with the continual intercession of the risen Lord. In the eucharist, Christ empowers us to live with him, to suffer with him and to pray through him as justified sinners, joyfully and freely fulfilling his will.

6. In Christ we offer ourselves as a living and holy sacrifice in our daily lives (Rom. 12:1; I Peter 2:5); this spiritual worship, acceptable to God, is nourished in the eucharist, in which we are sanctified and reconciled in love, in order to be servants of reconciliation in the world.

7. *United to our Lord and in communion with all the saints and martyrs, we are renewed in the covenant sealed by the blood of Christ.*

8. *Since the anamnesis of Christ is the very content of the preached Word as it is of the eucharistic meal, each reinforces the other. The celebration of the eucharist properly includes the proclamation of the Word.*

9. *The words and acts of Christ at the institution of the eucharist stand at the heart of the celebration; the eucharistic meal is the sacrament of the body and blood of Christ, the sacrament of his real presence. Christ fulfills in a variety of ways his promise to be always with his own even to the end of the world. But Christ's mode of presence in the eucharist is unique. Jesus said over the bread and wine of the eucharist: "This is my body ... this is my blood ... " What Christ declared is true, and this truth is fulfilled every time the eucharist is celebrated. The Church confesses Christ's real, living and active presence in the eucharist. While Christ's real presence in the eucharist does not depend on the faith of the individual, all agree that to discern the body and blood of Christ, faith is required.*

> *Commentary:*
>
> *Many churches believe that by the words of Jesus and by the power of the Holy Spirit, the bread and wine of the eucharist become, in a real though mysterious manner, the body and blood of the risen Christ, i.e., of the living Christ present in all his fullness. Under the signs of bread and wine, the deepest reality is the total being of Christ who comes to us in order to feed us and transform our entire being. Some other churches, while affirming a real presence of Christ at the eucharist, do not link that presence so definitely with the signs of bread and wine. The decision remains for the churches whether this difference can be accommodated within the convergence formulated in the text itself.*

C. The Eucharist as Invocation of the Spirit

1. *The Spirit makes the crucified and risen Christ really present to us in the eucharistic meal, fulfilling the promise contained in the words of institution. The presence of Christ is clearly the centre of the eucharist, and the promise contained in the words of institution is therefore fundamental to the celebration. Yet it is the Father who is the primary origin and final fulfilment of the eucharistic event. The incarnate Son of God by and in whom it is accomplished is its living centre. The Holy Spirit is the immeasurable strength of love which makes it possible and continues to make*

it effective. The bond between the eucharistic celebration and the mystery of the Triune God reveals the role of the Holy Spirit as that of the One who makes the historical words of Jesus present and alive. Being assured by Jesus' promise in the words of institution that it will be answered, the Church prays to the Father for the gift of the Holy Spirit in order that the eucharistic event may be a reality: the real presence of the crucified and risen Christ giving his life for all humanity.

> *Commentary:*
>
> *This is not to spiritualize the eucharistic presence of Christ but to affirm the indissoluble union between the Son and the Spirit. This union makes it clear that the eucharist is not a magical or mechanical action but a prayer addressed to the Father, one which emphasizes the Church's utter dependence. There is an intrinsic relationship between the words of institution, Christ's promise, and the epiklesis, the in-vocation of the Spirit, in the liturgy. The epiklesis in relation to the words of institution is located differently in various liturgical traditions. In the early liturgies the whole "prayer action" was thought of as bringing about the reality promised by Christ. The invocation of the Spirit was made both on the community and on the elements of bread and wine. Recovery of such an understanding may help us over-come our difficulties concerning a special moment of consecration.*

2. *It is in virtue of the living word of Christ and by the power of the Holy Spirit that the bread and wine become the sacramental signs of Christ's body and blood. They remain so for the purpose of communion.*

> *Commentary:*
>
> *In the history of the Church there have been various attempts to understand the mystery of the real and unique presence of Christ in the eucharist. Some are content merely to affirm this presence without seeking to explain it. Others consider it necessary to assert a change wrought by the Holy Spirit and Christ's words, in consequence of which there is no longer just ordinary bread and wine but the body and blood of Christ. Others again have developed an explanation of the real presence which, though not claiming to exhaust the significance of the mystery, seeks to protect it from damaging interpretations.*

3. *The whole action of the eucharist has an "epikletic" character because it depends upon the work of the Holy Spirit. In the words of the liturgy, this aspect of the eucharist finds varied expression.*

4. The Church, as the community of the new covenant, confidently invokes the Spirit, in order that it may be sanctified and renewed, led into all justice, truth and unity, and empowered to fulfil its mission in the world.

The Holy Spirit through the eucharist gives a fore-taste of the Kingdom of God: the Church receives the life of the new creation and the assurance of the Lord's return.

D. *The Eucharist as Communion of the Faithful*

1. The eucharistic communion with Christ who nourishes the life of the Church is at the same time communion within the body of Christ which is the Church. The sharing in one bread and the common cup in a given place demonstrates and effects the oneness of the sharers with Christ and with their fellow sharers in all times and places. It is in the eucharist that the community of God's people is fully manifested. Eucharistic celebrations always have to do with the whole Church, and the whole Church is involved in each local eucharistic celebration.

In so far as a church claims to be a manifestation of the whole Church, it will take care to order its own life in ways which take seriously the interests and concerns of other churches.

Commentary:

Since the earliest days, baptism has been understood as the sacrament by which believers are incorporated into the body of Christ and are endowed with the Holy Spirit. As long as the right of the baptized believers and their ministers to participate in and preside over eucharistic celebration in one church is called into question by those who preside over and are members of other eucharistic congregations, the catholicity of the eucharist is less manifest. There is discussion in many churches today about the inclusion of baptized children as communicants at the Lord's Supper.

2. The eucharist embraces all aspects of life. It is a representative act of thanksgiving and offering on be-half of the whole world. The eucharistic celebration demands reconciliation and sharing among all those regarded as brothers and sisters in the one family of God and is a constant challenge in the search for appropriate relationships in social, economic and political life (Matt. 5:23f; I Cor. 10:16f; I Cor. 11:20—22; Gal. 3:28). All kinds of injustice, racism, separation and lack of freedom are radically challenged when we share in the body and blood of Christ. Through the eucharist the all-renewing grace of God penetrates and restores human personality and dignity. The eucharist involves the believer in the central event of the world's history. As participants in the eucharist, therefore, we prove inconsistent if we are not actively participating in this ongoing restoration of the world's situation and the human condition. The eucharist shows us that our behaviour is inconsistent in face of the reconciling presence of God in human history: we are placed under continual judgment by the persistence of unjust relationships of all kinds in our society, the manifold divisions on account of human pride, material interest and power politics and, above all, the obstinacy of unjustifiable confessional oppositions within the body of Christ.

3. Solidarity in the eucharistic communion of the body of Christ and responsible care of Christians for one another and the world find specific expression in the liturgies: in the mutual forgiveness of sins; the sign of peace; intercession for all; the eating and drinking together; the taking of the elements to the sick and those in prison or the celebration of the eucharist with them. All these manifestations of love in the eucharist are directly related to Christ's own testimony as a servant, in whose servanthood Christians themselves participate. As God in Christ has entered into the human situation, so eucharistic liturgy is near to the concrete and particular situations of men and women. In the early Church the ministry of deacons and deaconesses gave expression in a special way to this aspect of the eucharist. The place of such ministry between the table and the needy properly testifies to the redeeming presence of Christ in the world.

E. The Eucharist as Meal of the Kingdom

1. The eucharist opens up the vision of the divine rule which has been promised as the final renewal of creation, and is a foretaste of it. Signs of this renewal are present in the world wherever the grace of God is manifest and human beings work for justice, love and peace. The eucharist is the feast at which the Church gives thanks to God for these signs and joyfully celebrates and anticipates the coming of the Kingdom in Christ (1 Cor. 11:26; Matt. 26:29).

2. The world, to which renewal is promised, is present in the whole eucharistic celebration. The world is present in the thanksgiving to the Father, where the Church speaks on behalf of the whole creation; in the memorial of Christ, where the Church, united with its great High Priest and Intercessor, prays for the world; in the prayer for the gift of the Holy Spirit, where the Church asks for sanctification and new creation.

3. Reconciled in the eucharist, the members of the body of Christ are called to be servants of reconciliation among men and women and witnesses of the joy of resurrection. As Jesus went out to publicans and sinners and had table-fellowship with them during his earthly ministry, so Christians are called in the eucharist to be in solidarity with the outcast and to become signs of the love of Christ who lived and sacrificed himself for all and now gives himself in the eucharist.

4. The very celebration of the eucharist is an instance of the Church's participation in God's mission to the world. This participation takes everyday form in the proclamation of the Gospel, service of the neighbour, and faithful presence in the world.

As it is entirely the gift of God, the eucharist brings into the present age a new reality which trans-forms Christians into the image of Christ and there-fore makes them his effective witnesses. The eucharist is precious food for missionaries, bread and wine for pilgrims on their apostolic journey. The eucharistic community is nourished and strengthened for confessing by word and action the Lord Jesus Christ who gave his life for the salvation of the world. As it becomes one people, sharing the meal of the one Lord, the eucharistic assembly must be concerned for gathering also those who are at present beyond its visible limits, because Christ invited to his feast all for whom he died. Insofar as Christians cannot unite in full fellowship around the same table to eat the same loaf and drink from the same cup, their missionary witness is weakened at both the individual and the corporate levels.

III The Celebration of the Eucharist

The eucharistic liturgy is essentially a single whole, consisting historically of the following elements in varying sequence and of diverse importance:
− *hymns of praise;*
− *act of repentance;*
− *declaration of pardon;*
− *proclamation of the Word of God − in various forms;*
− *confession of faith (Creed)*

- *intercession for the whole Church and for the world;*
- *preparation of the bread and wine;*
- *thanksgiving to the Father for the marvels of creation, redemption and sanctification (deriving from the Jewish tradition of the berakah);;*
- *the words of Christ's institution of the sacrament according to the New Testament tradition;*
- *the anamnesis or memorial of the great acts of redemption, passion, death, resurrection, ascension and Pentecost, which brought the Church into being;*
- *the invocation of the Holy Spirit (epiklesis) on the community, and the elements of bread and wine (either before the words of institution or after the memorial, or both; or some other reference to the Holy Spirit which adequately expresses the "epikletic" character of the eucharist);*
- *consecration of the faithful to God;*
- *reference to the communion of saints;*
- *prayer for the return of the Lord and the definitive revelation of his Kingdom;*
- *the Amen of the whole community;*
- *the Lord's Prayer*
- *sign of reconciliation and peace;*
- *the breaking of the bread;*
- *eating and drinking in communion with Christ and with each member of the Church*
- *final act of praise;*
- *blessing and sending.*

1. The best way towards unity in eucharistic celebration and communion is the renewal of the eucharist itself in the different churches in regard to teaching and liturgy. The churches should test their liturgies in the light of the eucharistic agreement now in the process of attainment.

The liturgical reform movement has brought the churches closer together in the manner of celebrating the Lord's Supper. However, a certain liturgical diversity compatible with our common eucharistic faith is recognized as a healthy and enriching fact. The affirmation of a common eucharistic faith does not imply uniformity in either liturgy or practice.

Commentary:

Since New Testament days, the Church has attached the greatest importance to the continued use of the elements of bread and wine which Jesus used at the Last Supper. In certain parts of the world, where bread and wine are not customary or obtainable, it is now sometimes held that local food and drink serve better to anchor the eucharist in every-day life. Further study is required concerning the question of which features of the Lord's Supper were unchangeably instituted by Jesus, and which features remain within the Church's competence to decide.

2. In the celebration of the eucharist, Christ gathers, teaches and nourishes the Church. It is Christ who invites to the meal and who presides at it. He is the shepherd who leads the people of God, the prophet who announces the Word of God, the priest who celebrates the mystery of God. In most churches, this presidency is signified by an ordained minister. The one who presides at the eucharistic celebration in the name of Christ makes clear that the rite is not the assemblies' own creation or possession; the eucharist is received as a gift from Christ living in his Church. The minister of the eucharist is the ambassador who represents the divine initiative and expresses the connection of the local community with other local communities in the universal Church.

3. Christian faith is deepened by the celebration of the Lord's Supper. Hence the eucharist should be celebrated frequently. Many differences of theology, liturgy and practice are connected with the varying frequency with which the Holy Communion is celebrated.

4. As the eucharist celebrates the resurrection of Christ, it is appropriate that it should take place at least every Sunday. As it is the new sacramental meal of the people of God, every Christian should be encouraged to receive communion frequently.

5. Some churches stress that Christ's presence in the consecrated elements continues after the celebration. Others place the main emphasis on the act of celebration itself and on the consumption of the elements in the act of communion. The way in which the elements are treated requires special attention. Regarding the practice of reserving the elements, each church should respect the practices and piety of the others. Given the diversity

in practice among the churches and at the same time taking note of the present situation in the convergence process, it is worthwhile to suggest:
- *that, on the one hand, it be remembered, especially in sermons and instruction, that the primary intention of reserving the elements is their distribution among the sick and those who are absent, and*
- *that on the other hand, it be recognized that the best way of showing respect for the elements served in the eucharistic celebration is by their consumption, without excluding their use for communion of the sick.*

The increased mutual understanding expressed in the present statement may allow some churches to attain a greater measure of eucharistic communion among themselves and so bring closer the day when Christ's divided people will be visibly reunited around the Lord's Table.

4.2 Bilateral dialogues in selection

In bilateral dialogues, it is not uncommon for the controversies existing between the two denominations holding the talks to hold centre stage at the deliberations. A comprehensive theological understanding of the Holy Communion, Eucharist and Holy Sacrifice cannot be achieved in this way. At the same time, the selection which follows here makes the richness of the thematic aspects that have already been considered in the ecumenical conversations impressively clear.

The dialogues presented here as examples are in alphabetical order of the churches involved, not in chronological sequence according to the time of the conclusion of a dialogue. For this reason, one cannot expected to recognise a stringent dialogue process. The form of presentation reflects the ecumenical reality: conversations on the subject of the Holy Communion, Eucharist and Holy Sacrifice take place on many levels – in international, regional and national contexts – without the individual bodies knowing about each other or indeed making reference to one another.

4.2.1 Anglican / Roman Catholic: clarifications on their statements

In September 1993, the Anglican / Roman Catholic International Commission (ARCIC) saw itself compelled to make clarifications with regard to the reception of individual statements in the dialogue documents submitted earlier.[3] The statements indicate that, from the point of view of the dialogue commission, helpful understandings have been reached on the understanding of the Eucharistic "sacrifice", on the interpretation of the presence of Jesus Christ in the meal in his memory, and on the question of ordination. Surprising and sobering were the reactions of the Roman Catholic Church in particular, which are in the background of the clarifications.

"14 When we speak of the death of Christ on Calvary as a sacrifice, we are using a term to help explain the nature of Christ's self-offering, a term which is not exhaustive of the significance of that self-offering."

"17 In several places the Final Report indicates its belief in the presence of the living Christ truly and really in the elements."

"18 A Reservation of the Blessed Sacrament is practised in both our churches for communion of the sick, the dying and the absent. (...) The difficulty is not with reservation of the sacrament but with the devotions associated with it which have grown up in the Western Church since the twelfth century outside the liturgical celebration of the Eucharist. To this day these devotions are not practised in the Eastern Churches, just as they had not been during the Church's first thousand years."

4.2.2 Free church and Roman Catholic

The Roman Cathol ic Church conducts many conversations; it seeks bilateral contacts with all confessional denominations. Each ecumenical conversation on the subject of Holy Communion and the Eucharist proceeds differently. The people who take part determine what happens. The thematic challenges vary accordingly.

(1) Baptist/Roman Catholic dialogue

The report on the results of the international discussions between the Roman Catholic Church and the Baptist World Alliance between 2006 and 2010 has been published under the title "The Word of God in the Life of the Church".[4] It is a study report by those who participated in these dis-

---

[3] Cf. Clarifications of Certain Aspects of the Agreed Statements on Eucharist and Ministry by the ARCIC (September 1993)
[4] The Word of God in the Life of the Church. A Report of International Conversations between the Catholic Church and the Baptist World Alliance (2006-2010)

cussions. It is not a binding statement of the Roman Catholic Church or the Baptist World Alliance.

The starting point of the conversations under the overall theme *"The Word of God in the Life of the Church"* is that Jesus Christ, the Word of God made flesh, draws us into the Trinitarian communion with God, from which the communion of the Church emerges, so that the *koinonia* of the Church participates in the *koinonia* of the Trinity. It then goes on to explore what Baptists and the Catholic Church can say in common fundamentally regarding Holy Scripture, tradition, the sacraments/ordinances, the role of Mary in the life of the Church, ecclesiastical order and the ministry of oversight (episkopé).

In Part IV, under the heading: *Baptism and the Holy Communion or Eucharist: The Visible Word of God in the koinonia of the Church,* the relationship of faith and sacraments, which is central for Baptists as well as other Protestant free churches, is dealt with. Therefore, the dialogue on the Holy Communion between Baptists and the Roman Catholic Church is also of great importance for other Protestant free churches such as the International Federation of Free Evangelical Churches.

Sacraments, called 'ordinances' by most Baptists, are unanimously understood as "making visible" the Word of God, whereby divine grace and human faith – as in hearing the Word of God – are interwoven in the events of the sacraments. There is thus a coherence between sacraments/ordinances and the proclamation of the Word of God.

The central relationship between God's work of grace and the confession of faith in the sacraments is described by both traditions in agreement with the following words:

(No. 77) *The terms 'sacrament' and 'ordinance' express both God's own gift of love (agape) and faith-filled human response. The sacrament/ordinance becomes the point of intersection between a divine commitment and a human commitment, where the priority belongs to God's salvific act.*

Moreover, it can be declared jointly: *(No. 91) The essential relationship between faith and the sacrament/ordinance involves the faith of the individual believer and the community. (No. 92) Both traditions affirm that faith is visibly expressed through both its public profession and through the community celebrating worship. The Catechism of the Catholic Church refers to the sacraments as 'sacraments of faith'. ... Sacraments are the word of God expressed in sacramental form. They are received in faith through a free acceptance of God's gift. Thus there is no sacramental event without faith. The sacraments express acceptance of God's word and are, thereby, a profession of faith. Faith is always both personal faith and ecclesial faith.*

Baptists and Catholics agree that the Holy Communion and the Eucharist belong to the being of the church and are celebrated in obedience to Jesus' command: "Do this in remembrance of me" (1 Cor 11:24; Lk 22:19).

(No. 117) Baptists and Catholics agree that the church cannot be the church without the Eucharist/Lord's Supper. Likewise, there can be no Eucharist/Lord's Supper without the church, for it is never a private or individual act, but one always done in the context of a community.

Similarities are also noted with regard to the order of service for the celebration of Holy Communion and the liturgy of the Eucharist: *(No. 121) There is a trinitarian pattern in the order of worship of the Eucharist/Lord's Supper. In it the church prays to the Father in thanksgiving (eucharistia) as Jesus did, recalling God's acts in the history of salvation; it remembers, celebrates and participates (anamnesis) in the death and resurrection of the Son; and it calls upon the Holy Spirit (epiclesis) to make the presence of Christ real to his disciples.*

(2) Mennonite / Roman Catholic Dialogue

The theme of the International Dialogue between the Catholic Church and the Mennonite World Conference was for many years: Called Together to be Peacemakers.[5] The dialogue begins with a common hermeneutic of history as the basis for a joint re-reading of history and an important step towards healing the often painful memories of the respective communities.

Conversations on the nature of the church, as well as the sacraments and ordinances, are placed in the context of a shared hermeneutic of history, a shared commitment to peace and the healing of memory.

The Holy Communion and the Eucharist are part of a comprehensive process of rapprochement and reconciliation between the churches. It is also a significant factor for the faithful in their commitment to the body of Christ and in following Jesus Christ. And it is the commitment and mission

---

[5] Called Together to be Peacemakers. Report of the International Dialogue between the Catholic Church and Mennonite World Conference 1998 – 2003

of the Church and the faithful to be servants of reconciliation, peace and justice for the world.

Despite differing terminology – the expression congregational ordinance, or ordinance for short, is used in Anabaptist-Mennonite theology instead of sacrament – the Catholic Church and the Mennonite Church agree (No. 128) *that baptism and the Lord's Supper have their origin and point of reference in Jesus Christ and in the teachings of Scripture. Both regard the celebration of these sacraments/ordinances as extraordinary occasions of encounter with God's offer of grace revealed in Jesus Christ.*

Regarding the Holy Communion and the Eucharist, Mennonites and the Catholic Church agree that (No. 134) *the risen Christ is present at the celebration of the Eucharist/Lord's Supper. Christ is the one who invites to the meal; he is present in the faithful who are gathered in his name; and he is present in the proclaimed Word.*

Although there are divergences, including understanding of the manner of the presence of Jesus Christ, substantial agreements are noted regarding significant aspects of the Holy Communion or Eucharist: (No. 133) *1) Both hold that the celebration of the Eucharist/Lord's Supper is rooted in God's marvellous gift of grace made available to all people by virtue of the suffering, death, and resurrection of Jesus Christ. 2) We agree that the Lord's Supper/Eucharist recalls the suffering, the death, and the resurrection of Christ. 3) We agree that the meal provides an important occasion for the acknowledgement of our sinfulness and for receiving grace and forgiveness. 4) Both celebrate the Eucharist/Lord's Supper for the nourishing of Christian life; for the strengthening of the church's sense of mission; and for the conforming of our communities to the body of Christ in order to be ministers of reconciliation, peace and justice for the world (cf. 1 Cor 11:17-32; 2 Cor 5:16-21). 5) Both celebrate the Lord's Supper/Eucharist in the spirit of Christian hope, as a foretaste of the heavenly banquet anticipated in the coming kingdom of God.*

(3) Methodist / Roman Catholic Dialogue

The ninth report of the International Dialogue between the World Council of Methodist Churches and the Roman Catholic Church of 2011 deals with the theme: *Encountering Christ the Saviour: Church and Sacraments.*[6]

---

[6] Encountering Christ the Saviour: Church and Sacraments. Ninth Report of the In-

The basis of a common approach to the sacramental reality of the Eucharist is the common understanding of the biblical teaching of the priestly nature of Christ, the unity between Christ and his sacrifice, which happened once for all but continues forever, and the unity of Christ and the Church. Methodologically enriching and significant is that, in addition to the common biblical-theological reflection, hymns and songs of the Methodist tradition are also included to describe the self-giving and presence of Jesus Christ in the sacraments and in the Eucharist.

Under the heading in Chapter 3: *"II. We enter together more deeply into the saving mystery of Christ"*[7], beliefs are described which Methodists and Catholics together hold to be true and through which a high degree of agreement can be reached regarding the Eucharist as the sacramental commemoration of Christ's saving death and resurrection.

These include that the saving mystery of Christ is wholly God's gift, that Christ is present in the Eucharist, and that believers and the baptised receive a share in the self-giving of Jesus Christ: (No. 94) *Any communion or participation in the saving mystery of Christ is itself an effect of God's grace, and totally dependent on Christ's prior offering of himself for us.*

With regard to the Eucharist, in so far as it involves a sacrifice, it can be declared jointly:

(No. 93) *The Eucharist is the celebration of Christ's full, perfect and sufficient sacrifice, offered once and for all, for the whole world. It is a memorial which is not a mere calling to mind of a past event or of its significance, but the Church's effectual proclamation of God's mighty act in Christ. In this celebration we really share in Christ's offering of himself in obedience to the Father's will.*

The Eucharist as an act of thanksgiving implies that the baptised and believers are participants in, not spectators at, the Eucharist, and that the thanksgiving of the Church and the faithful is always a grace-filled response to God's gift: (No. 110): *We can respond only through grace, because God has empowered us to act. Taking part in the Eucharist should lead to God's baptized, priestly people being transformed by the Holy Spirit ever more truly into the likeness of Christ, and to a more radical following and imitating of Christ, but also to a deeper participation in*

---

ternational dialogue between the World Methodist Council and the Roman Catholic Church. Durban, 2011

[7] Ibid. from No. 89

Christ and in all that he has done for us, so that we "enter together more deeply into the saving mystery of Christ".

The centre of a common understanding of the eucharistic sacrifice is the conviction that Christ unites his Church with his self-offering: (No. 134) *"It is the risen and ascended Christ himself, by the power of the Holy Spirit, who unites his once-for-all yet eternal self-giving and ours as one single offering, pleaded and presented to the Father and accepted by him. We come to the Eucharist to enter into Christ's self-gift to the Father, and are taken "through him, with him and in him", in the unity of the Holy Spirit, to the Father."*

4.2.3 Lutheran/Roman Catholic

Dialogues were able to result in far-reaching rapprochements, and in some cases also agreements, on issues that had been disputed between Lutherans and Roman Catholics since the 16th century. This applies to understandings about the presence (of the body and blood) of Christ in the sacrament, the reception under both forms, the understanding of the sacrifice in the Eucharist and the leadership of the worship celebration of the sacrament, as well as to the understanding of "sola fide" and "ex opere operato". The following quotations from some of the dialogue documents lead on further:

> *In the sacrament of the Lord's supper Jesus Christ, true God and true man, is present wholly and entirely, in his body and blood, under the signs of bread and wine.*[8]

Catholic and Lutheran Christians together recognize that in the Eucharist Jesus Christ "is present as the crucified who died for our sins and rose again for our justification, as the once-for-all sacrifice for the sins of the world". This sacrifice can be neither continued, nor repeated, nor replaced, nor complemented; but rather it can and should become effective ever anew in the midst of the congregation. There are different interpretations among us regarding the nature and extent of this effectiveness.[9]

All those who celebrate the Eucharist in remembrance of Him are incorporated in Christ's life, passion, death and resurrection. They receive the fruit

---

[8] The Eucharist – Report of the Lutheran-Roman Catholic Commission on Unity (1978) – No. 16
[9] Ibid. No. 56

of Christ's offering his life and thereby of the entire reconciling saving act of God. In the Passover meal of the new covenant, they are freed and united with God and with one another. So they give thanks "for all his mercies, entreat the benefits of his passion on behalf of the whole church, participate in these benefits and enter into the movement of his self-offering". In receiving in faith, they are taken as His body into the reconciling sacrifice which equips them for self-giving (Romans 12:1) and enables them "through Jesus Christ" to offer "spiritual sacrifices"(1 Peter 2:5) in service to the world. Thus is rehearsed in theLord's Supper what is practised in the whole Christian life. "With contrite hearts we offer ourselves as a living and holy sacrifice, a sacrifice which must be expressed in the whole of our daily lives".[10]

The decisive achievement was to overcome the separation of sacrificium (the sacrifice of Jesus Christ) from sacramentum (the sacrament). If Jesus Christ is really present in the Lord's Supper, then his life, suffering, death, and resurrection are also truly present together with his body, so that the Lord's Supper is "the true making present of the event on the cross." Not only the effect of the event on the cross but also the event itself is present in the Lord's Supper without the meal being a repetition or completion of the cross event. The one event is present in a sacramental modality.[11]

Lutherans and Catholics confess together that Christ's self-sacrifice is performed historically once for all by His suffering, dying, and resurrection—from Maundy Thursday night to Easter morning (triduum paschale). His self-sacrifice "to the point of death, even death on a cross" (Phil. 2:8) is distributed in the Eucharist as a life-giving reality.[12]

Through the consecratory words and prayer of thanksgiving, a word of faith addressed to the Father, the bread and wine become the body and blood of Christ by the action of the Holy Spirit. At Holy Communion we eat the flesh of Christ and drink his blood. In the epiclesis we also ask that we may receive Holy Communion worthily in faith and receive strength to

---

[10] Ibid. No. 36
[11] From Conflict to Communion – Lutheran-Catholic Common Commemoration of the Reformation in 2017 (2013) – No. 159
[12] Final Report of the Theological Conversations between the Churches Associated within the International Lutheran Council and the Roman Catholic Church in: Lutheran Theological Review 33 (2021), p. 27

love our neighbours. The truth affirmed in faith about the Eucharist must shape the content and form of the liturgy.[13]

In all Lutheran and Catholic orders of the Mass, both old and new, the words of institution, or the dominical words of consecration, are central. There is also no doubt that these words are perceived as the most important part of the Mass. They are surrounded by several symbolic actions that underline their significance. The need for an epiclesis has been less clear. In the old Roman canon, which today is the First Eucharistic Prayer, there is a prayer asking for the help of the power of God to transform the bread and wine into a spiritual gift. Although the Holy Spirit is not explicitly mentioned, this prayer has subsequently been understood as an epiclesis. Historically, the epiclesis could also be placed either before or after the words of consecration, and it has then been a prayer asking for the transformation of either the elements or the communicants.[14]

We agree that the sign of communion is more complete when given under both kinds, since in that form the sign of the eucharistic meal appears at its clearest. The validity of the Eucharist is based on the consecration and on Christ's presence in the species, not on the manner in which they are used. Therefore, those who receive only the consecrated bread also receive the whole Christ. In Lutheran practice communion under both kinds is the norm because Christ used both bread and wine when he instituted the Eucharist. Catholics generally agree concerning the merits of communion under both kinds in principle, but the practical application varies and communion in many local Churches is predominantly administered under one kind. However, in the Catholic particular Churches in the Nordic countries communion is often administered under both kinds. In view of our common understanding of the theological principle the practice, which in any case is not absolute, is not Church-dividing. 156 The condemnations of the Reformation era (DS 1653; Epit. 7.22; SD 7.107) are thus not applicable today.[15]

Since the question of the presidency at the eucharistic celebration is of great ecumenical significance, it is an important commonality that the di-

---

[13] Evangelical Lutheran Church of Finland/Catholic Church in Finland, Communion in Growth. Declaration on the Church, Eucharist, and Ministry. A report from the Lutheran-Catholic Dialogue Commission for Finland, Helsinki 2017, No. 117.
[14] Ibid. No. 120
[15] Ibid. No. 129

alogue established the need of a minister commissioned by the church: "Catholic and Lutheran Christians are of the conviction that the celebration of the eucharist involves the leadership of a minister appointed by the church."[16]
Nevertheless, Catholics and Lutherans still understand the office of ministry differently.[17]

4.2.4 Oriental Orthodox/Roman Catholic

The Eastern Churches are three large families of churches: the Orthodox Churches, the Oriental Orthodox Churches and the Eastern Catholic Churches. Today, more than 60 churches worldwide belong to this Orthodox tradition. The three groups each have eucharistic communion only within their church family.

Two agreements should be pointed out here as examples because they point the way for future ecumenical togetherness:

(1) Joint Declaration by Pope John Paul II and Patriarch Ignatius Zakka I Iwas on 23 June 1984

The first joint declaration on the reception of the sacraments dates back to 1984. On 23 June, the Syrian Orthodox and Roman Catholic Churches agreed in the Vatican on a pastoral declaration. In this declaration, Patriarch Mar Ignatius Zakka I Iwas and Pope John Paul II permitted the faithful to receive the sacraments from the priests of the other church, if it was impossible to find access to a priest of their own church. These include the Sacrament of Penance, Eucharist and Anointing of the Sick. In the document, the Pope and the Syrian Orthodox Patriarch refer to the common faith of both churches. Confusions and schisms that occurred did not touch "the substance of the faith", they had rather only arisen because of "differences in terminology and culture" and due to their own forms of expression. "We find today no real basis for the sad divisions and schisms." Common to both churches is the belief in the perfect divinity and perfect humanity of Christ, says the statement from both churches.

This statement from 1984 forms a major exception to start with.[18]

---

[16] The Eucharist, No. 65
[17] From Conflict to Communion, No. 161
[18] https://www.vatican.va/content/john-paul-ii/en/speeches/1984/june/documents/hf_jp-ii_spe_19840623_jp-ii-zakka-i.html

(2) Another document, in this case from 2001, is also exemplary and forward-looking. This document is reproduced in full below. The Holy Apostolic Catholic Assyrian Church of the East (Assyrian Church of the East) and the Babylonian Patriarchate of the Chaldeans (The Chaldean Catholic Church), which is united with Rome, agreed in 2001 on guidelines for admission to the Eucharist. This very remarkable agreement includes a number of interesting points. The Assyrian Church of the East is considered to be a church which, as the "Nestorian" church, was considered for centuries by almost the entire ecumenical community to be heretical, because of its Christology. The Assyrian Church of the East is considered to have no words of institution in its celebration of the Holy Communion, i.e. in the Anaphora of Addai and Mari, so that its liturgy has been called "deficient". At the beginning of the 21st century, it was able to be reconciled and enter into eucharistic communion with its breakaway "daughter church", namely the Chaldean Catholic Church. This agreement between the Assyrian Church of the East and the Roman Catholic Church was certainly only brought about by years of historical, liturgical and ecumenical-theological dialogue.

GUIDELINES FOR ADMISSION TO THE EUCHARIST BETWEEN THE CHALDEAN CHURCH AND THE ASSYRIAN CHURCH OF THE EAST
Given the great distress of many Chaldean and Assyrian faithful, in their motherland and in the diaspora, impeding for many of them a normal sacramental life according to their own tradition, and in the ecumenical context of the bilateral dialogue between the Catholic Church and the Assyrian Church of the East, the request has been made to provide for admission to the Eucharist between the Chaldean Church and the Assyrian Church of the East. This request has first been studied by the Joint Committee for Theological Dialogue between the Catholic Church and the Assyrian Church of the East. The present guidelines subsequently have been elaborated by the Pontifical Council for Promoting Christian Unity, in agreement with the Congregation for the Doctrine of Faith and the Congregation for the Oriental Churches.

1. PASTORAL NECESSITY
The request for admission to the Eucharist between the Chaldean Church and the Assyrian Church of the East is connected with the particular geographical and social situation in which their faithful are actually living.

Due to various and sometimes dramatic circumstances, many Assyrian and Chaldean faithful left their motherlands and moved to the Middle East, Scandinavia, Western Europe, Australia and Northern America. As there cannot be a priest for every local community in such a widespread diaspora, numerous Chaldean and Assyrian faithful are confronted with a situation of pastoral necessity with regard to the administration of sacraments. Official documents of the Catholic Church provide special regulations for such situations, namely the Code of Canons of the Eastern Churches, can. 671, §2-§3 and the Directory for the Application of Principles and Norms of Ecumenism, n. 123.

2. ECUMENICAL RAPPROCHEMENT
The request is also connected with the ongoing process of ecumenical rapprochement between the Catholic Church and the Assyrian Church of the East. With the 'Common Christological Declaration', signed in 1994 by Pope John Paul II and Patriarch Mar Dinkha IV, the main dogmatic problem between the Catholic Church and the Assyrian Church has been resolved. As a consequence, the ecumenical rapprochement between the Chaldean Church and the Assyrian Church of the East also entered a further phase of development. On 29 November 1996 Patriarch Mar Raphaël Bidawid and Patriarch Mar Dinkha IV signed a list of common proposals with a view to the re-establishment of full ecclesial unity among both historical heirs of the ancient Church of the East. On 15 August 1997 this program was approved by their respective Synods and confirmed in a 'Joint Synodal Decree'. Supported by their respective Synods, both Patriarchs approved a further series of initiatives to foster the progressive restoration of their ecclesial unity. Both the Congregation for the Oriental Churches and the Pontifical Council for the Promotion of Christian Unity support this process.

3. THE ANAPHORA OF ADDAI AND MARI
The principal issue for the Catholic Church in agreeing to this request, related to the question of the validity of the Eucharist celebrated with the Anaphora of Addai and Mari, one of the three Anaphoras traditionally used by the Assyrian Church of the East. The Anaphora of Addai and Mari is notable because, from time immemorial, it has been used without a recitation of the Institution Narrative. As the Catholic Church considers the words of the Eucharistic Institution a constitutive and therefore indis-

pensable part of the Anaphora or Eucharistic Prayer, a long and careful study was undertaken of the Anaphora of Addai and Mari, from a historical, liturgical and theological perspective, at the end of which the Congregation for the Doctrine of Faith on January 17th, 2001 concluded that this Anaphora can be considered valid. H.H. Pope John Paul II has approved this decision. This conclusion rests on three major arguments.

In the first place, the Anaphora of Addai and Mari is one of the most ancient Anaphoras, dating back to the time of the very early Church; it was composed and used with the clear intention of celebrating the Eucharist in full continuity with the Last Supper and according to the intention of the Church; its validity was never officially contested, neither in the Christian East nor in the Christian West.

Secondly, the Catholic Church recognises the Assyrian Church of the East as a true particular Church, built upon orthodox faith and apostolic succession. The Assyrian Church of the East has also preserved full Eucharistic faith in the presence of our Lord under the species of bread and wine and in the sacrificial character of the Eucharist. In the Assyrian Church of the East, though not in full communion with the Catholic Church, are thus to be found "true sacraments, and above all, by apostolic succession, the priesthood and the Eucharist" (U.R., n. 15). Secondly, the Catholic Church recognises the Assyrian Church of the East as a true particular Church, built upon orthodox faith and apostolic succession. The Assyrian Church of the East has also preserved full Eucharistic faith in the presence of our Lord under the species of bread and wine and in the sacrificial character of the Eucharist. In the Assyrian Church of the East, though not in full communion with the Catholic Church, are thus to be found "true sacraments, and above all, by apostolic succession, the priesthood and the Eucharist" (U.R., n. 15).

Finally, the words of Eucharistic Institution are indeed present in the Anaphora of Addai and Mari, not in a coherent narrative way and ad litteram, but rather in a dispersed euchological way, that is, integrated in successive prayers of thanksgiving, praise and intercession.

4. GUIDELINES FOR ADMISSION TO THE EUCHARIST
Considering the liturgical tradition of the Assyrian Church of the East, the doctrinal clarification regarding the validity of the Anaphora of Addai and Mari, the contemporary context in which both Assyrian and Chaldean

faithful are living, the appropriate regulations which are foreseen in official documents of the Catholic Church, and the process of rapprochement between the Chaldean Church and the Assyrian Church of the East, the following provision is made:

1. *When necessity requires, Assyrian faithful are permitted to participate and to receive Holy Communion in a Chaldean celebration of the Holy Eucharist; in the same way, Chaldean faithful for whom it is physically or morally impossible to approach a Catholic minister, are permitted to participate and to receive Holy Communion in an Assyrian celebration of the Holy Eucharist.*

2. *In both cases, Assyrian and Chaldean ministers celebrate the Holy Eucharist according to the liturgical prescriptions and customs of their own tradition.*

3. *When Chaldean faithful are participating in an Assyrian celebration of the Holy Eucharist, the Assyrian minister is warmly invited to insert the words of the Institution in the Anaphora of Addai and Mari, as allowed by the Holy Synod of the Assyrian Church of the East.*

4. *The above considerations on the use of the Anaphora of Addai and Mari and the present guidelines for admission to the Eucharist, are intended exclusively in relation to the Eucharistic celebration and admission to the Eucharist of the faithful from the Chaldean Church and the Assyrian Church of the East, in view of the pastoral necessity and ecumenical context mentioned above.*
Rome, July 20th, 2001[19]

4.2.5 Orthodox/Roman Catholic

Following the historic meeting of Pope Paul VI and Patriarch Athenagoras I in Jerusalem in 1964, there were further meetings between the representatives of the Roman Catholic Church and the Orthodox Church. In 1979, an official dialogue commission was set up to conduct dialogues between the two churches at the world level. Analogously, dialogues between the two churches were and continue to be conducted in Germany as

---

[19] http://www.christianunity.va/content/unitacristiani/en/dialoghi/sezione-orientale/chiesa-assira-dell-oriente/altri-documenti/testo-in-inglese.html

well. In 1980, for example, a joint commission was established between the German Bishops' Conference and the Greek Orthodox Metropolitan Church of Germany, which has met twice a year since 1981. In addition to practical questions of how Christians of both confessions work and meet together, the commission also deals with theological issues. In 1989, the joint commission of the Greek Orthodox Metropolitan Church and the Roman Catholic Church in Germany published a report entitled "The Eucharist of the One Church. Liturgical Tradition and Ecclesial Communion, Bonn 1989".[20] Among other things, this report includes in German translation documents prepared by the Joint International Commission for Theological Dialogue between the Roman Catholic and Orthodox Churches. "The Mystery of the Church and the Eucharist in the Light of the Mystery of the Holy Trinity," Munich 1982; "Faith, Sacraments and the Unity of the Church," Bari 1987; and "The Sacrament of Order in the Sacramental Structure of the Church with Particular Reference to the Importance of Apostolic Succession for the Sanctification and Unity of the People of God", Valamo 1988.[21]

The document "The Eucharist of the One Church. Liturgical Tradition and Ecclesial Communion, Bonn 1989" consists of two parts. The first part, chapters 1-4, deals with the theme "The Eucharist as a legacy for the building up and unity of the Church". In the second part, Chapters 5-14, the common liturgical tradition and its range of variation are shown by means of some examples from the history of liturgy.

The observations presented here are intended to make us aware of how fruitful mutual "give and take" can be for the churches. The newly discovered common ground commits us to common witness and common service. It has been the express wish of the members of the Commission that the statements reproduced in this document should not merely be read, but lived.

"10. The full symbolism of the Communion gifts of the body and blood of the Lord. The Communion tradition of both churches agrees that the legacy of the "body given" and the "blood poured out" is realised in the preparation

---

[20] Die deutschen Bischöfe Ökumene-Kommission 8, – Die Eucharistie der einen Kirche Dokumente des katholisch-orthodoxen Dialogs auf deutscher und internationaler Ebene, 27. Mai 1989, 3rd expanded edition, Bonn 1995, 7-24.

[21] Ibid, 25-58.

and offering of bread and wine, in the proclamation of the Lord's words and in the epiclesis over both kinds and in the reception of both kinds – at least by the priests celebrating. In these three liturgical procedures, the participation of the faithful has been weakened in the course of liturgical history. The faithful, who once provided and donated bread and wine themselves for the eucharistic sacrifice, usually as "the work of their own hands" and at the same time as "(gifts) to God belonging to God", were often no longer able to do this themselves after the churches had in many cases changed to using bread and wine of a special kind for the Eucharist. The common thanksgiving, which according to the testimony of the early Fathers is sealed by the responses and the final Amen of the Anaphora, was obscured from the early Middle Ages onwards by the fact that the Anaphora was wholly or partly either performed as a silent prayer – in the West, or drowned out by choral singing – in the East. In the occidental liturgy, communion under both kinds was abolished for the faithful by the introduction not only of a special kind of sacrificial bread and wine, but also of non-crumbling azymes in order to avoid dishonouring even the smallest particles, and by reserving chalice communion for the priest. This restriction of the Communion of the faithful to the form of bread in Western practice is admittedly far-reaching and can no longer be understood simply as a peculiarity of the Roman rite. The regulations since Vatican Council II have not retained the withholding of the lay chalice, but have expressly provided for the Communion of the faithful under both forms for special occasions, such as Masses at weddings or at small group retreats, and also at the Easter Vigil, and do not rule out an extension of this practice in the future.

11. The use of unleavened bread in the celebration of the Eucharist. In this context, the aforementioned use of unleavened bread – the azymes – introduced into the Western liturgies towards the end of the first millennium, which was intended to avoid dishonouring the sanctified gifts, can also be seen as a restriction of the symbolism of the eucharistic gifts. In the Western view, however, the azymes appeared to be a means of emphasising the historical symbolism of the sacrificial bread for salvation, since Christ, given that the Last Supper took place on the date and under the circumstances of the Jewish Passover meal, had himself used azymes for the foundation of the Lord's Supper. However, despite all the efforts of exegetes, it remains unclear to this day whether Jesus, in accordance with the Passover character of his Last Supper as attested by the Synoptics, actually observed the date and certain ritual preconditions of the Passover meal, or whether, according to the chronology of John's Gospel, his Last Supper was a meal celebrated in advance and without azymes. Today, the right encounter with the liturgy of the respective sister

church offers the chance to experience in the Orthodox liturgy the Passion symbolism of the Eucharist celebration as it is expressed with the Proskomedia; while it is equally impressive to see how the use of azymes in the Mass of the Roman Catholic Church enables the faithful to experience the Eucharist as the new and true Passover meal."[22]

In the final chapter 14 it is explicitly pointed out that the dialogue cannot deal with the unity of the sacrament of the Eucharist and the other sacraments in the two churches without clarifying the question of unity in confession and belief, which forms the basis and prerequisite for all other questions and issues. Therefore, the overcoming of all differences that still stand in the way of unity of faith must be sought in the light of this fact.

> "14. Eucharistic tradition and ecclesial communion. The fundamental commonality of eucharistic tradition in the Orthodox and Roman Catholic Churches, which has always been linked to the mutual recognition of the integrity of the eucharistic mystery, raises the question of when this common tradition can again lead to eucharistic koinonia, which was exemplarily expressed in the undivided Church of the first millennium. Both churches agree today that even similar eucharistic traditions and a complete consensus of faith in relation to the Eucharist cannot in themselves support a eucharistic communion between the churches, since faith is indivisible and a communion of Eucharist and church can only be justified in a commonality encompassing all confessional issues – including those of ecclesiology. It is one of the basic principles of Orthodox-Catholic dialogue that "unity in faith is a prerequisite for unity in the sacraments and especially in the Holy Eucharist". The overcoming of all differences still standing in the way of unity in faith must be sought in the light of the fact that the eucharistic celebration of both churches confesses a communion of faith which is not limited to eucharistic and sacramental theological content. As the eucharistic Anaphora testify, the celebration of the Eucharist is related to the Triune God and his activity in salvation history. In this celebration, the church proclaims "what she is: the mystery of the Trinitarian Koinonia ", the "dwelling of God with men" (Rev 21:3).
> On behalf of the Joint Commission of the Greek Orthodox Metropolis and the Roman Catholic Church in Germany: Metropolitan Agoustinos of Germany and Exarch of Central Europe / Paul-Werner Scheele Bishop of Würzburg,

---

[22] Ibid, 16-18

Chairman of the Ecumenical Commission of the German Bishops' Conference Bonn, 27 May 1989".[23]

4.2.6 Reformed/Roman Catholic

Today, new paths are being trodden in the ecumenical dialogues – which also have implications for the question of the significance of the controversies surrounding the topics of the Holy Communion, Eucharist and Holy Sacrifice. The focus is directed more towards the practical level. If one makes a realistic assessment of the rapprochements that might conceivably be achieved at the institutional level regarding the doctrines of the ordained ministry, one is confronted with the problem of what joint projects may nonetheless be possible from a Christian perspective. As a result, joint concerns in social and ethical areas on the global level command the most attention. One example which proves this observation is the report on the fourth phase of the Reformed / Roman Catholic international dialogue (2011-2015), which was published under the title "Justification and Sacramentality: The Christian Community as an Agent for Justice"[24]. One section in it is entitled "Eucharist and Justice in the World":

(65) It is with regret that we must acknowledge that, even though we agree on the implications of the Eucharist for justice, our two communions still cannot celebrate the Eucharist together. The reasons for this situation have not yet been addressed by dialogue between our churches at the international level, though we hope that this will be taken up in the future. With this in mind we are nevertheless able to say together the following.

(66) The Eucharist by its very nature leads to sharing and caring for the poor and disadvantaged. (...) As the objects of God's love, men and women become subjects of charity, they are called to make themselves instruments of grace, so as to pour forth God's charity and to weave networks of charity. (...)

(67) The connection between the Eucharist and love was also nicely underlined by some of the earliest Christian writers.

---

[23] Ibid, 20-21
[24] http://www.christianunity.va/content/unitacristiani/en/dialoghi/sezione-occidentale/alleanza-mondiale-delle-chiese-riformate/dialogo-internazionale-cattolico-riformato/documenti-di-dialogo/testo-in-inglese.html

(68) The Eucharist points out, in a most eminent way, what it means to be a Christian. Its celebration necessarily implies a certain way of life. Regarding justice, the Eucharist recalls and manifests that, in Christ, the righteousness of God has been revealed, as a gift and human response. In the offering of his body and the shedding of his blood, a new order has been definitively established. Each celebration of the Eucharist introduces us into the dynamic of justification, reconciliation and re-creation of humankind. But the witness character of the sacramental symbols does not end with human re-creation. Immersed in the waters of baptism and transformed by sharing the manna of Christ, fruit of the earth, and work of human hands, we are also thereby called to be responsible stewards of the environment. Our sharing of a meal must also be extended to the responsibility to safeguard that the earth be habitable for all. In the face of so many structures and mechanisms of injustice and exclusion, the Eucharist should be a true sign of the coming kingdom of God.

4.2.7 Independent Evangelical Lutheran Church in ecumenical dialogues

In recent years, the SELK has participated in various ecumenical dialogues.

1. DNK-LWB – SELK

Doctrinal discussions took place between the German National Committee of the Lutheran World Federation and the SELK from 2008 to 2010. The preliminary result was:

> "With regard to the initial question about the possibility of granting eucharistic hospitality, the following result was achieved: 'Despite the differences mentioned, both churches consider […] the granting of pastorally responsible eucharistic hospitality to be possible.'"

Admittedly, different principles apply here: the United Evangelical Lutheran Church in Germany (VELKD) had already declared such eucharistic hospitality in principle in 1981, while the SELK for its part provides for the granting of eucharistic hospitality only "in special situations" of a pastoral nature.

2. SELK – UEK

There was a significant meeting between the SELK and the Union of Evangelical Churches (UEK) on the occasion of the commemoration of the Reformation in 2017, which coincided with the 200th anniversary of the Prussian Union of Churches. As a result, it could be jointly stated that both churches are essentially rooted in the Reformation of the 16th century. This mutual recognition was valid irrespective of the theological and political conflicts and divisions that led to the emergence of both church bodies in the 19th century.

It is considered acceptable in the UEK that in larger church fellowships (UEK, EKD, CPCE) different confessions have validity, although they can neither easily nor completely be brought into harmony with one another, while in the SELK confessional differences among existing churches is seen as an obstacle to the formation of binding church unity. The disagreement at this point shows that clarifications are still pending".

3. ILC – PCPCU

An informal academic dialogue was concluded between the International Lutheran Council (ILC) and the Pontifical Council for Promoting Christian Unity (PCPCU) in 2019.

With regard to the *Eucharist*, the following points were formulated in common; they discovered:

> *"consensus in the real and essential presence of Christ's body and blood in the consecrated elements;*
> *consensus in emphasising the necessity of the consecration of the elements of bread and wine with the words of institution in a Christian assembly, the distribution of these elements which are the body and blood of Christ after the consecration, communion, and the proclamation of Christ's death;*
> *convergences in the understanding of the presence of the sacrifice of Christ in the Lord's Supper;*
> *convergences in the understanding of the connection between God's action and human involvement in the liturgy of the Church. "*

Ecumenical Tasks in the Horizon of Intentional Catholicity were jointly formulated. These include: 1 "Mutual perception and appreciation of the different character of our ecclesiastical-theological mentalities", 2 "Joint efforts to produce language that is able to communicate each side's intentions" and 3 "Intensified understanding of the divine and ecclesial actions in their relationship to each other."

4. SELK – UEK – VELKD.

The trialogue between the SELK, the UEK and the VELKD is nearing completion. From the *perspective of the SELK,* it can be said for the time being that in adoptingup the *Mutual Recognition of Baptism* (Magdeburg Declaration of 2007), the *realisation* of the reality of the church in the respective other churches has been achieved. This also concerns the dimension of "spiritual ecumenism". On the other hand, no common understanding has yet been reached on the preconditions and practices of full ecclesial communion.

4.3 Lutheran, Reformed and United Churches in Europe: "Leuenberg Agreement" (1973)

In the 16th century, the theological differences in the teachings of Martin Luther and Huldrych Zwingli on Holy Communion were so weighty that the Lutheran and Reformed confessions that formed at the beginning of the Reformation period did not celebrate together at the Lord's Table even in the following generations. Since then, there have been many theological discussions with the aim of establishing a union of the Reformation churches. Since the middle of the 20th century, the conviction grew that the agreements reached in the doctrine of the Lord's Supper between the Lutheran, Reformed and United church communities in Europe are so far-reaching that the remaining differences could not justify exclusion from fellowship at the Lord's Supper. Since 1973, therefore, table and pulpit fellowship exists between the Protestant churches which agree to the Leuenberg Agreement of 1973 and are today united in the "Community of the Protestant Church in Europe" (CPCE). We document here excerpts from the "Leuenberg Agreement"[25], which was the basis for further doctrinal conversations.

---

[25] https://www.leuenberg.eu/documents/

Leuenberg Agreement (1973)

1. On the basis of their doctrinal discussions, the churches assenting to this Agreement – namely, Lutheran and Reformed Churches in Europe along with the Union Churches which grew out of them, and the related pre-Reformation Churches, the Waldensian Church and the Church of the Czech Brethren – affirm together the common understanding of the Gospel elaborated below. This common understanding of the Gospel enables them to declare and to realize church fellowship. Thankful that they have been led closer together, they confess at the same time that guilt and suffering have also accompanied and still accompany the struggle for truth and unity in the Church.

2. The Church is founded upon Jesus Christ alone. It is he who gathers the Church and sends it forth, by the bestowal of his salvation in preaching and the sacraments. In the view of the Reformation it follows that agreement in the right teaching of the Gospel and in the right administration of the sacraments is the necessary and sufficient prerequisite for the true unity of the Church. It is from these Reformation criteria that the participating churches derive their view of church fellowship as set out below.

(...)

18. In the Lord's Supper the risen Jesus Christ imparts himself in his body and blood, given up for all, through his word of promise with bread and wine. He thus gives himself unreservedly to all who receive the bread and wine; faith receives the Lord's Supper for salvation, unfaith for judgement.

19. We cannot separate communion with Jesus Christ in his body and blood from the act of eating and drinking. To be concerned about the manner of Christ's presence in the Lord's Supper in abstraction from this act is to run the risk of obscuring the meaning of the Lord's Supper.

20. Where such a consensus exists between the churches, the condemnations pronounced by the Reformation confessions are inapplicable to the doctrinal position of these churches.

(...)

29. In the sense intended in this Agreement, church fellowship means that, on the basis of the consensus they have reached in their understanding of the Gospel, churches with different confessional positions accord each other fellowship in word and sacrament and strive for the fullest possible co-operation in witness and service to the world.

4.4 Ecumenical Working Group of Protestant and Catholic Theologians (ÖAK): "Together at the Lord's Table"

The study "Together at the Lord's Table"[26], presented by Protestant and Roman Catholic theologians on the basis of much preparatory work in other ecumenical writings, proves that from the beginning of Christianity there was and still is a variety of liturgical forms of thanksgiving for the life, death and resurrection of Jesus Christ. The remembrance of Jesus Christ in its significance for those living as his followers today is the meaning of the eucharistic celebration. In the Holy Spirit, Jesus Christ becomes present with his gift of life for us in the broken bread and the shared cup. Reconciliation, fellowship and eschatological hope are experienced in a symbolic act that has an effect beyond the experience.

Taking account of biblical, theological, historical and pastoral insights, the ÖAK has formulated a plea that individual Christians, trusting in the presence of Jesus Christ, may also participate in the liturgical celebrations of other confessions if their situation gives reason to do so – justified, for example, biographically by challenges in a mixed-denominational family or motivated locally in the confessional diaspora. This plea is linked to the concept that new joint liturgies should not be planned, but rather that one should appreciate the different forms of celebration that have emerged in the history of the churches, learn from each other, talk to one other about objections, and discover in the process the existent breadth of the one spiritual fellowship in the life of worship today.

There have long been efforts in the ecumenical movement to determine the common elements in the eucharistic liturgical commemoration of the death, resurrection and life of Jesus Christ. The idea, taken up in the Lima liturgy, of seeking a form in which all confessional concerns are taken into account is of lasting significance. However, the statement by the ÖAK follows a different road: respecting the ecumenical convergences already achieved in the understanding of the Holy Communion and the Eucharist, in the understanding of the church and in the doctrines of ministry, as described in the ÖAK's study, it is proposed to allow oneself to be invited by Jesus Christ himself to the forms of worship which have already long

---

[26] Cf. "Together at the Lord's Table", see note 3

been practised in a confessional community, trusting in his presence there. The study "Together at the Lord's Table" presents a broad scientific basis to demonstrate which commonalities in the understanding of the Holy Communion and the Eucharist, as well as in the understanding of church and ministry, have already been recognised in ecumenical dialogues. Jesus Christ has promised his presence to all who gather in his name, listen to his word and encounter him as the risen and exalted Lord in the eucharistic meal. The experience of fellowship in Holy Communion and Eucharist is a source of hope for the unity of the churches.

The critical reception of the study "Together at the Lord's Table", especially on the Roman Catholic world church level, is documented and reflected in a second volume by the "Ecumenical Working Group of Protestant and Catholic Theologians".[27] This second volume of the study, which will be followed by a third in 2023, will also provide bibliographic references for scholarly reception. The discussion about the statement and its reasoning will be continued. An insight into the overall structure of the study, the joint testimony and the formulated plea is provided by the excerpts reproduced here:

TOGETHER AT THE LORD'S TABLE
A statement by the Ecumenical Working Group of Protestant and Catholic Theologians

1. Introduction
(1.1) The Ecumenical Working Group of Protestant and Catholic Theologians, which was founded in Paderborn in 1946 under the episcopal chairmanship of Lorenz Jaeger and Wilhelm Stählin, has dealt frequently and intensively with the topic "Holy Communion/Eucharist and Ministry" from an ecumenical perspective. In numerous ecumenical dialogues on the national and international level, convergences have been achieved, which should now be compiled and combined. In recent times, other ecumenical bodies have also attempted to summarise the positions on the topics of understanding of the Church, Holy Communion/Eucharist and Ministry.
(1.2) Some years ago, ecumenical hermeneutics opened the harvest period for the fruits of previous ecumenical dialogues. This concern is combined with the determination to follow up the relevant theological understandings with practical consequences, to be agreed upon in a binding way. In our context, the "Joint Declaration on the Doctrine of Justification" (1999) can function

---
[27] Cf. Together at the Lord's Table, Vol. II, see note 4

both as guide and warning. Efforts to examine the state of the dialogues "in via" – on the way to church communion – were received with widespread approval. At the same time, it was regretted that these efforts apparently failed to bring consequences at the level of local ecumenical life in the congregations, organisations and families.

(1.3) The presentation below is guided by the following ecumenical interests: (1) Provision should be made for the fact that the theological dialogues conducted ecumenically in the past decades have succeeded in coming to such a degree of understanding in all issues connected with the Holy Communion/Eucharist which had been controversially discussed in the 16th century that it is no longer permissible to regard the remaining differences as church-dividing. (2) It is established and affirmed that there is unanimous agreement on the theological meaning of the Holy Communion/Eucharist, and that on this basis the diversity of liturgical traditions is appreciated. (3) It should become clear that all theological disciplines (exegetical, historical, systematic and practical) enable their own respective access to the topic of the Holy Communion/Eucharist, which are given consideration in the general theological understanding of the Holy Communion/Eucharist developed here; the expectation is that in each case the current state of research is represented. (4) The past and present diversity of liturgical practice in the celebration of the Holy Communion/Eucharist is the constant point of reference for all these reflections. Their aim is to recognise and support all efforts which affirm the theological meaning and share on this basis the concern to celebrate Holy Communion/Eucharist together. (5) The presentation focuses on the Western tradition and makes only occasional reference to Orthodoxy; rapprochements in the whole ecumenical spectrum can only be achieved gradually. However, ecumenism will always have to strive for a multilateral perspective if it is not to lose sight of its goal of church unity in the sense of common confessional tradition.

(1.4) In our title we consciously refer to the joint celebration of the Holy Communion/Eucharist. Eucharist is giving thanks and praise for God's action as Creator and Redeemer. At the Last Supper this divine promise of his presence is given by words and symbolic acts for all times. Together we are called to the living memorial of this legacy of Jesus Christ.

(1.5) Thematically our study is structured as follows: The starting point of the reflections is a common testimony regarding the theological meaning of the celebration of the Holy Communion/Eucharist (Section 2). The biblical-theological foundation demonstrates the various ways in which the Lord's Supper was celebrated by the early Christians, as witnessed by the New Testa-

ment texts, resulting from the events of Jesus' death and resurrection (Section 3). A tour through the history of the forms of celebration helps to recognise the diversity of liturgical practice (Section 4). The ecumenical controversies and the convergences achieved are described (section 5). Special attention is paid to the question of the office of ministry at the Holy Communion/Eucharist (Section 6). The relationship between church communion and Eucharistic fellowship has to be considered (Section 7). Finally there is a plea to open the denominational Lord's Supper to Christians from other traditions (Section 8).

2. Common testimony
In accordance with the spiritual character of the Holy Communion/Eucharist, we begin these remarks with a common testimony.
(2.1) Jesus Christ promised his presence to those who come together in his name (cf. Mt 18:20). He is in their midst, even if only two or three gather in his name. He becomes present to them as they worship him by hearing, singing and praying. He unites with them when people receive baptism in the name of the Father, the Son and the Holy Spirit, making them members of his body. In his body and blood, given to all, he offers himself to them as they trust in his promise and partake of bread and wine in the Eucharistic celebration of Holy Communion.
(2.2) The promise of his presence transcends and encompasses confessional boundaries and demarcations standing in the way of Christendom's visible unity – it is profoundly ecumenical. It underlies every single step in ecumenism. Wherever Catholic, Orthodox, Lutheran, Reformed, Anglican, Baptist and Methodist Christians are gathered in his name, Christ fulfils his promise to be there in their midst. They are united in Christ long before they have agreed on the concrete forms of their unity and made concrete arrangements for their togetherness.
(2.3) It is in accordance with the will of Jesus Christ that believers pray together in his name and gather for ecumenical services of worship, irrespective of their different denominational affiliations and backgrounds. The strongest expression of ecumenism in church and parish life is when members of various Christian churches celebrate services jointly and pray the Lord's Prayer together. This takes place today in many parts of the world with gratifying determination, quite naturally and unselfconsciously. Ecumenical services trusting in the promise of the presence of Jesus Christ are pacemakers of unity. "Welcome one another ... just as Christ has welcomed you, for the glory of God" (Rom 15:7). Precisely here the apostle's appeal should come into its own.
(2.4) The Christian churches are unanimously certain that the presence of Jesus Christ is expressed most intensely and profoundly in the fellowship at

the Lord's Table and that the encounter with him in the celebration of the Holy Communion/Eucharist comes to pass in a concentration that cannot be surpassed under earthly conditions. That is why the separation at the Lord's Table is felt to be particularly painful. It is one of the most urgent goals of ecumenical understanding to overcome this.

(2.5) The mutual recognition of baptism, as expressed by many member churches of the Council of Christian Churches in Germany in 2007 in the "Magdeburg Declaration", can be regarded as a decisive step on the way to fellowship at the Lord's Table. The decisive passage states: "Baptism, as participation in the mystery of Christ's death and resurrection, means rebirth in Jesus Christ. Whoever receives this sacrament and affirms God's love in faith is united with Christ and simultaneously with his people of all times and at all places. As a sign of the unity of all Christians, baptism is the bond with Jesus Christ, the foundation of this unity. Despite differences in our understanding of church, we share a basic understanding on baptism." Since the act of baptism constitutes their membership in the body of Christ, those who are baptised enter into unity with Jesus Christ and thus into unity with his people. The "basic understanding on baptism" is stronger than the differences in the understanding of the church. It is to be clarified whether a common "basic understanding" may prove to emerge with regard to Holy Communion/Eucharist, enabling – in analogy to the recognition of baptism – a mutual recognition of the respective liturgical forms of celebrating the Lord's Supper and their theological content and thus justifying an invitation to mutual participation. This text seeks to examine this possibility.

(2.6) The celebration of Holy Communion/Eucharist unites us with Jesus Christ and at the same time with his believers of all times and at all places. This fellowship with God in the Spirit of Jesus Christ encompasses and transcends space and time. The celebration of the Holy Communion/Eucharist takes place in the communio sanctorum, uniting the living and the dead in resurrection hope.

(...)

8. A plea for participation in the celebrations of the Holy Communion/Eucharist with attention to the respective liturgical traditions
(8.1) The Ecumenical Working Group of Protestant and Catholic Theologians considers the practice of mutual participation at the celebrations of the Holy Communion/Eucharist, respecting each other's liturgical traditions, to be theologically well-founded. It is in particular a pastoral requirement for interdenominational families. Up to now, the solutions have been most unsatisfactory

both in individual cases and as a general rule. Our current plea implies the recognition of the respective liturgical forms as well as the leadership ministry obtaining in the congregation which invites persons of other denominations baptised in the name of Jesus Christ to join in their service. This suggestion does not look for a new form of Eucharistic liturgy specially agreed in each case and going beyond the traditions that have developed historically. For the purposes of the practice we propose, it is assumed that baptism is recognised as a sacramental bond of faith and a necessary condition for participation. Under this condition, those authorities can also be respected for whom prayers are offered in the Roman Catholic liturgy (i.e. the local bishops and the Pope). Such an invitation to participation in traditions that are regularly practised implicates that ecumenical conversations will be continued with a view to the future; they will serve to seek answers to the question of how comprehensive visible unity of the Church of Jesus Christ will take shape in earthly time and in human environments.

We base our plea on arguments from the Bible and history, from systematic theology and practical theology, which have been explained in detail above. The main considerations are as follows:

(8.2) The content of the celebrations of the Holy Communion/Eucharist can today be described by mutual ecumenical agreement. Their reason and purpose are identical: in paschal hope, we celebrate the memorial of Jesus' redeeming life and death as instituted by him, in a liturgical action in which his presence can be experienced in the proclamation of the Word and in the meal by the power of the Holy Spirit. This is why Jesus' words spoken over the bread and wine (verba testamenti) are at the centre of the Eucharistic liturgy: Christians proclaim the death of Jesus, believing that he lives and hoping that he will come for the salvation of the world. The inner preparation of the believers by repentance and contrition before celebrating God's revealed mystery of his reconciling being is a constitutive element in all denominational liturgies, even if in various specific forms.

(8.3) Many ecumenical talks have deepened the realisation that differences in theological contents and forms of liturgical celebration of the Holy Communion/Eucharist must not stand in the way of mutual participation in the celebration of this sacramental mystery. Official doctrinal texts in the Roman Catholic tradition mostly ascribe the division at the Eucharistic meal to differences in the understanding of the presiding ministry. In this sense, they insist on the maintenance of participation in the apostolic mission. In the meantime, it has been possible to reach a common, differentiated understanding of

the apostolic succession in numerous national and international ecumenical dialogues, enabling the view that the ordained ministry in its varying confessional forms stands on the apostolic foundation. In the New Testament scriptures, the term "apostle" not only describes the twelve disciples, but also the other witnesses to the resurrected Christ. The assumption that there has been an unbroken chain of laying on of hands from the apostles to the present day was motivated by apologetics from the very beginning and cannot be proven historically. The connection between the apostolic origins and the faith life of today's Christian communities is made and maintained by the power of the Spirit of God. This connection comes through the proclamation of the gospel in Word and Sacrament in accordance with Scripture with the aid of the Spirit of God. It is still necessary today to examine every ecclesiastical office to see whether the criteria of the promised working of the Spirit are fulfilled in the exercise of the ministry, building and fortifying the local congregation, consoling troubled consciences, taking care of the needy and strengthening the resurrection hope. The present ecumenical understanding attaches special importance to the office of regional supervision (the episkopé) – whether as a person or appointed in a presbyterial-synodal fashion – for the examination of these criteria. The care already exercised in ecumenism today in the training, advancement and differentiation of spiritual vocations, as well as in the transfer of ministry in ordination with prayer and laying on of hands – all intended to protect the proclamation of the gospel – entitles us to trust that the ecumenical partners are aware of their responsibility before God as they regulate the transfer of ministry.

(8.4) Ecumenical sensitivity demands that, when organising liturgical celebrations, one should make allowance for the concerns of the other denominations as far as this is possible in the sense of one's own tradition. In this context, the insights gained in the ecumenical talks can make a real difference in practice. The two gestures instituted by Jesus at the meal are to be understood as a strongly expressive two-fold action by which he represents his will to make a new covenant despite the sin of humankind. It conforms to the will of Jesus when all those at the meal eat the broken bread and drink from the one cup. According to ecumenical conviction, the presence of Jesus Christ in the offerings is promised as long as their proper use is recognisable; that is the reason for treating the offerings with care. Individual liturgical prayers should be examined to avoid misunderstandings regarding the concept of sacrifice; they should not give rise to the impression that the congregation is sacrificing Jesus Christ for God, for it is rather God who considers the gifts of the congregation – whether material or spiritual – worthy of serving the celebration

of Jesus Christ's gift of his life. In future ecumenism it will be helpful to come to an understanding on binding details and to agree on certain basic rules of liturgical practice.

(8.5) Many baptised people are shaped by their own confessional tradition and therefore hardly familiar with how the Holy Communion/Eucharist is celebrated in other churches. The celebration of this sacrament can not only be regarded as a high point in the faith life in church communions that already exist. Experience suggests that the experience of Eucharistic communion in the celebration of the Lord's Supper is also a source of hope on the way to the goal desired by God: the full visible unity of the Church in the presence of the Kingdom of God. On the route to this goal, people who are already sacramentally connected in baptism can draw strength from the celebration of the meal in order to stand the tests of everyday life and find encouragement in serving their neighbours in the world.

5 Holy Communion – Eucharist – Holy Sacrifice

Joint Statement of the German Ecumenical Study Committee (DÖSTA)

The publication of the text "Together at the Lord's Table" by the Ecumenical Working Group of Protestant and Catholic Theologians has triggered a broad discussion on the question of communion between different Christian churches, confessions and denominations. Since the document predominantly considers Protestant and Catholic perspectives, the German Ecumenical Study Committee (DÖSTA) set itself the task of developing a multi-confessional view. This was done principally at a conference of the Association of Christian Churches in Germany (ACK), which took place in Pforzheim-Hohenwart on September 29, 2021. The draft of a working group was adopted by the DÖSTA in its meeting on 8/9 April 2022 in the version presented here.

Holy Communion – Eucharist – Holy Sacrifice
Legacy and remembrance of Jesus Christ – considered multilaterally

1. The concern

The German Ecumenical Study Committee (DÖSTA) of the Council of Churches in Germany (ACK) is grateful for the growing number of voices in national and worldwide ecumenical contexts calling for a joint theological effort on the questions of "Eucharist – Holy Communion – Holy Sacrifice". Ecumenical dialogues over many years have already led to understandings in terms of language and content. In the context of a conference as well as a survey, all member churches of the ACK have addressed the ecumenical significance of the topic. The DÖSTA would like to strengthen the theological efforts for understanding on "Eucharist – Holy Communion – Holy Sacrifice" by examining multilateral ecumenism. The reason for this objective is to be found in Jesus' words on the Lord's Supper, to which Paul bears witness: "Do this in remembrance of me" (1 Cor 11:24f). The Johannine tradition of the so-called High Priestly Prayer of Jesus before his death draws a connection between people's belief in Jesus Christ and the way in which they live, confessing and following him in reconciliation and fellowship (cf. Jn 17:20f). The mission of Jesus Christ himself forms the root of joint reflection on helps and hindrances to overcoming divisions in the very understanding and celebration of the "sacrament of unity" (which is named differently according to the denomination: Holy Communion among Protestants, Eucharist among Catholics, or Holy Sacrifice among the Orthodox).

2. Joint witness

The basis of Christian action is trust in God's action in Jesus Christ. Together, Christians have trusted in the presence of Jesus Christ in their midst in their liturgical celebrations for centuries. Together, Christians listen to the same words of the Holy Scriptures that tell of God's action towards Israel and in the Christian community. Together, Christians experience the stories of Jesus' life as the reason for their hope of healing, guidance, reconciliation and consolation. Seeing Jesus Christ's willingness, in the face of his own death, to bear witness to God's covenant faithfulness and desire for relationship to sinners is the common ground of Christian faith. The *one* paschal hope unites all Christians. We live in eschatological expectation and are aware of temporal needs on the way to eternity. In this earthly time, we as Christians are Christ's ambassadors. We are prepared to be sent into the world around us, where people hunger and thirst for justice, peace and the integrity of creation. Together, we look to those in need, whether near or far. Together, we want to preserve the natural resources for future generations. The eucharistic celebrations of all Christian churches thus combine the remembrance of Jesus Christ with the mission to today's world. As believers in Christ, we celebrate our common Easter hope and are active in a variety of ministries.

3. Mutual awareness of the diversity of forms of celebration

Ever since the foundation of local Christian communities, many different liturgical forms have developed to celebrate thanksgiving for the life, death and resurrection of Jesus Christ. The remembrance of Jesus Christ in its significance for his followers today is the central content of the eucharistic celebration. The form of the celebration serves to express this meaning. In the Holy Spirit, Jesus Christ, who gave his life for us, becomes present in the bread that is broken and the cup that is shared. Reconciliation with God and other people, fellowship with God and fellow humans, and eschatological hope are experienced in a service of worship which has a lasting effect and commitment.

In ecumenical fellowship, it is important for Christians to meet one another trustingly in the forms of celebration that have come down through history, so that they can learn from one another, speak to one another and discover the broad extent of spiritual fellowship which already exists in worship today. The aim should be to preserve, share and strengthen the diversity of worship that characterises our common ecumenical tradition with its richness of liturgies, which has attracted increased attention during the Covid pandemic.

4. Controversies concerning the fellowship at the liturgical meal

In their official rules, the churches presently hold different positions in determining the prerequisites for experiencing fellowship in the celebration of the Holy Communion, Eucharist and Holy Sacrifice. The crucially controversial point is the extent to which a communion of churches has to exist before eucharistic communion can be granted.

The Orthodox tradition tends to be the most stringent judge when it comes to the prerequisite of communion in faith and ecclesiastical matters for eucharistic communion. In principle, Orthodoxy cannot invite people to celebrate the Divine Liturgy together out of consideration for the church's official position. Nonetheless, the following also applies to Orthodoxy: "For freedom Christ has set us free" (Gal 5:1), as Paul proclaims. In the celebration of Holy Communion, the Eucharist and the Holy Sacrifice, we can therefore allow the faith to prevail that is active in love.

Since some Orthodox churches see no possibility of recognising baptisms performed in the Western churches, they also not give no further consideration to communion at the Lord's Table. However, certain Orthodox and Oriental Orthodox churches in Germany have signed the Magdeburg Declaration on the mutual recognition of baptism, thus entering on their own promising path.

The doctrinal texts of the Western churches also advocate a close connection between church communion and eucharistic communion. At the same time, the Roman Catholic tradition describes exceptions in which participation in the celebration is possible for reasons of pastoral concern. Here the principle applies that, with regard to the aim of the ecumenical movement, the unity of the church(es) must also be respected within institutions; on the other hand, the grace to be had from common worship for individual believers in Christ and their families "sometimes commends this practice" (cf. UR 8,4). Accordingly, exceptions are foreseen.

The connection between communion of faith and Holy Communion is not unknown to the Protestant tradition in German regional churches, but here there is a different emphasis. If there is a common understanding of the Lord's Supper, all believers in Christ are invited to the celebration. Jesus Christ himself extends this invitation in the Holy Spirit. On the basis of the recognition that the remaining differences are not sufficient to divide the church, the Communion of Protestant Churches in Europe (Leuenberg Agreement, 1973) states that there is a solid basis for table and pulpit fellowship between the Reformation churches. From the outset it was agreed that further discussions should deepen the common theological positions.

In other churches there is a wide range of different positions. The Old Catholic Church invites all baptised Christians to partake in communion if they share its belief in the presence of Jesus Christ in the signs of bread and wine.

Protestant free churches usually celebrate an "open Lord's Supper", to which all believers in Christ are invited in Jesus' name – regardless of their baptism or church affiliation. They leave it to the conscience of those attending the service to decide whether to participate or not (in the sense of 1 Cor 11:28: Examine yourselve, and only then eat of the bread and drink of the cup). In the Methodist Church, which understands the Lord's Supper as a means of grace and thus also as a call to faith, all those are invited who "all who love Jesus … and seek to live in peace with one another." The Salvation Army and Quakers respect the sacraments, but do not administer them themselves.

Other churches, such as the Independent Evangelical Lutheran Church (SELK), are convinced that fundamental differences between the churches in matters of faith, doctrine and confession prevent the communion of churches and fellowship at the Lord's Table. For them and other churches, communion of churches and sacraments is the fruit and affirmation of the churches' communion in faith, doctrine and confession. Nevertheless, even churches which in principle advocate exclusivity of admission to Holy Communion, Eucharist and Holy Sacrifice pay attention ro eucharistic hospitality based on pastoral care, for example in the case of interdenominational marriages.

In certain areas, there are noticeable differences between the agreements which have been reached in ecumenical dialogues and the practice in the churches. From a historical perspective, we can recognise the following divisive theological issues in the realm of the Latin Western Church. In the 16th century, disputes between the Lutheran and Reformed traditions on the theological understanding of the Lord's Supper weighed more heavily than those between the Roman Catholic and Lutheran sides. The two Reformation groups fought in particular over the question whether the presence of Jesus Christ at the Supper were (also) bodily – as the Lutherans would have it – or (solely) spiritual – according the Reformed view. The critical question levelled at the Roman Catholic side was whether the favoured doctrine of transubstantiation was not based more on philosophy than on theology. For Orthodoxy, the bread is changed into the body of Christ and the wine into the blood of Christ. The sacrifice of Christ is not repeated, but made real in a liturgical and sacramental way; therefore Orthodoxy cannot accept that it is merely to be symbolically understood. An understanding of the "real and symbolic" presence of Jesus Christ may be seen as a possible road to convergence between the approaches to the presence of the crucified and exalted Christ, which are otherwise so diverse.

However, there is a need for clarification of further points: for example on the question of baptism as a necessary prerequisite for the celebration of the Lord's Supper; a more precise definition of what is to be understood by "real presence"; the stipulation that only ordained ministers be allowed to lead the celebration of the Lord's Supper; communion under both forms; certain prayer texts which imply that the church is offering Jesus Christ as a sacrifice to God; and the way in which the eucharistic gifts are treated that are left over after the service.

5. On ecumenical understanding and deepening of the theme

It is obvious that many Christians do not know the liturgical practice of the other churches, and have perhaps never even visited a service of another denomination. Meeting each other in worship is a prerequisite for deepening ecumenical engagement. Going to see the church buildings of other denominations, or looking at the list of their services in newsletter, bulletin boards and digital media, can help to strengthen ecumenical awareness. There is still much to discover in ecumenical solidarity: how the services are held, what the churches look like, the pictures on the walls and the places for scripture readings and sermons.

Since the time of the Early Church, the celebration of the Lord's Supper, as a weekly Passover, has been particularly related to the observance of the Lord's Day, Sunday, the memorial day of Jesus Christ's resurrection. There is widespread ecumenical convergence in the conviction that Sunday is to be sanctified. The celebration of Holy Communion, the Eucharist and the Holy Sacrifice is consensually defined in ecumenism as a celebration of the memory (memoria/anamnese) of Christ's sacrifice on the cross, of his voluntary gift of life on the cross as the consummation of his earthly pro-existence, as a celebration of the *Memoria Passionis* (in remembrance of the suffering and death of Jesus Christ). Today, it is up to all Christian traditions to reflect together on their experiences with regard to the intervals (daily, weekly, fortnightly, monthly or other rhythms) in which the services are held. New forms are emerging that are less oriented towards pre-determined times, but rather take account of situations and events.

We advocate a continuation and intensification of ecumenical discussion of the meaning (not merely the form) of the Eucharist, Holy Sacrifice and Holy Communion. This includes important topics such as: eucharistic "sacrifice" (in connection with the soteriological relevance of Jesus' death on the cross); human models to describe the true presence of Jesus Christ in the meal; remembrance of the dead against the background of eschatological purification. The question of who presides at the celebration and is authorised to do so also requires further discussion. Furthermore, we believe it is possible and desirable to actively encourage people to get to know the other forms of worship. We therefore consider it right to extend and accept reciprocal invitations to Sunday worship and to festivals at other churches.

6. Ecumenical sensitivity in planning and performing the service

In the interests of the ecumenical movement, all services should be celebrated in an ecumenically sensitive way. It is our common ecumenical conviction that God's Spirit brings about unity. When celebrating Holy Communion, the Eucharist or the Holy Sacrifice, one must pay attention to this central aspect of epicletic prayer (the invocation of the Holy Spirit) with regard to an ecumenically sensitive form of denominational worship. We recommend our churches to examine the practice of worship in their own church and denomination to see whether they are exercising the necessary ecumenical consideration and, where appropriate, make corrections to the current practice.

We recommend our churches to encourage those responsible for the liturgy to ensure and promote strong participation by members of the congregation. It should be made clear that it is those who believe in Christ and hope in him – that is to say, the whole congregation – who are celebrating Holy Communion, Eucharist or Holy Sacrifice. Explicitly, the congregation are worshipping together, holding the service jointly. One person is officially appointed to lead the celebration, but is recognisably part of the congregation.

Liturgy focuses on the biblical scriptures and prayer texts and on the liturgical actions. These elements should be handled in such a way that they really come into their own and can speak for themselves. Holy Scripture unites Christianity, the Bible is the common document of faith. We therefore recommend that Christians from other traditions be involved as lectors in the readings from the Old and New Testaments.

The Creed and the Lord's Prayer are the confession and prayer that unite the Christian churches. At the same time, they are texts which are familiar from church services and the Bible. They unite Christianity and mark the connection between baptism and the Eucharist. The Creed is a part of the baptismal liturgy, as is the Lord's Prayer.

We recommend that other Christian churches be remembered in the prayers; especially in the context of an ecumenical event this should be a matter of course.

Communion under both forms corresponds to the commission of remembrance of Jesus Christ which is recorded in the Bible. Christ, whose death and resurrection are remembered here and now, becomes present in this celebration under the two forms of bread and wine (or grape juice). We recommend our churches to take steps to ensure that liturgical practice corresponds to this reality. That means that communion should normally be distributed and received under both forms. The same is true for ensuring that the leftover gifts of the table are handled in a worthy fashion.

7. Further suggestions

The DÖSTA strongly advocates that the member churches of the Council of Churches in Germany (ACK) continue to address the theology as well as the liturgical practice of Holy Communion, Eucharist and Holy Sacrifice with ecumenical sensitivity. Such an undertaking is of particular importance because differences still exist, for example, in the understanding of the Real Presence, of the sacrificial character and the leadership of the celebration. At present, it is important to name these differences clearly, while at the same time respecting them mutually, yet still working to overcome them. There is often too little knowledge about the rapprochements that have already been achieved on these topics in ecumenical dialogues. The DÖSTA believes it would be particularly promising to take a multilateral approach, aimed at receiving, complementing and expanding the discussions which were predominantly bilateral up to now.

The DÖSTA therefore supports the endeavour to promote encounters and conversations within and between the denominations on the questions of Eucharist, Holy Communion and Holy Sacrifice:

We strongly encourage congregations to become more familiar with each other's liturgical practice at the local level by attending each other's services. Worshipping jointly, listening to God's Word, singing and praying together, is a spiritual enrichment, even if it does not include eucharistic fellowship. The DÖSTA considers it worthwhile to cultivate the exchange of views concerning the significance of this celebration in people's everyday lives. It is possible to gain experience in ecumenical sensitivity. The DÖSTA recommends that the member churches of the ACK provide appropriate materials in the future, especially for the liturgical celebration.

The DÖSTA advocates support for international multilateral ecumenical meetings on the subject at the theological level. This could lead to a continuation of the Lima Convergence Statements on "Baptism, Eucharist and Ministry" adopted by the Faith and Order Commission of the World Council of Churches in 1982.

The DÖSTA understands these recommendations as an encouragement to our churches to develop concrete practical measures, enabling them to deal locally with the topic of Holy Communion, Eucharist and Holy Sacrifice in a way that concentrates on experience, spiritual support and solid theology.

Text of a resolution passed at the meeting of the DÖSTA on 9 April 2022 in Ludwigshafen

6 "Come and see!"

A concern of the 3rd Ecumenical Kirchentag 2021 in Frankfurt

Julia Meister und Christoph Stender

6.1 A look back at the Third Ecumenical Kirchentag (ÖKT)

Longing for communion at the Lord's Table

During the preparations for the 3rd Ecumenical Kirchentag (Church Congress – ÖKT) there were already intensive ecumenical discussions and ongoing mutual efforts to overcome the separation of the denominations at their respective meal celebrations.

So this ÖKT was also confronted with the question of whether progress could at long last be made in fulfilling the longing for a joint communion service of the confessions.

The hope for progress was strengthened by the publication "Together at the Lord's Table"[1], which appeared a few months before the Ecumenical Kirchentag and was prepared by the Ecumenical Working Group of Protestant and Catholic Theologians (ÖAK).

Based on insights from biblical theology, history and pastoral care, the authors have formulated a plea for mutual invitations to liturgical celebrations held and structured in confessional responsibility, trusting in the presence of Jesus Christ.

The Presidium of the 3rd ÖKT decided to support this statement and invited the Christian communities in Frankfurt, but also from other places, to

---

[1] Cf. Together at the Lord's Table, see note 3

organise Communion and Eucharist celebrations on the Saturday evening of the 3rd ÖKT in an ecumenically sensitive way in the spirit of this plea.

Under the motto "Come and see!", the doors of Frankfurt's churches were opened wide on this Saturday. They invited people to take part confidently in the services of the other denomination, and thus to get to know the traditions of the other denominations and to experience for themselves: it is Christ himself who invites us to his table.

"Katholikentag" and "Kirchentag"

Protestant and Catholic Christians in Germany usually celebrate in alternate years their lay people's congresses lasting several days: the "Kirchentag" (organised by Protestants) and the "Katholikentag" (held by Catholics). These festivals of faith with tens of thousands of participants take place in various cities that are capable of accommodating and handling large numbers of visitors. The umbrella organisations are the "German Protestant Kirchentag" or the "Central Committee of German Catholics", and the programme is then in the hands of active Christian groups, congregations, associations and other organisations. From Wednesday evening to Sunday midday, Christians come together to hold worship services, discuss current political and social issues, exchange views on theological and ecclesiastical questions and to experience cultural events; in short: to get to know each other as Christian brothers and sisters, to join one another and work together for common goals.

Ecumenical Kirchentags

The last Protestant Kirchentag, which was the 37th to be held in Germany, took place in Dortmund in 2019, and the previous year the 101st Katholikentag had taken place in Münster. The chronological sequence of these congresses had already been interrupted by the first Ecumenical Kirchentag (ÖKT) in Berlin in 2003 and the second in Munich in 2010, and this was also the case for the third time in 2021, when the 3rd Ecumenical Kirchentag was held in Frankfurt/Main. Like the others, this Kirchentag was organised by the two "mainstream" Christian churches and with the participation of many other Christian churches and communities (multilateral ecumenism).

Eucharist and Celebration Supper

The Ecumenical Kirchentags in Berlin and Munich had already included the so-called "Feierabendmahl", a celebration supper, which originated in the Protestant tradition and was first celebrated at the 1979 Kirchentag in Nuremberg. Since then, it has been customary for hosts and guests to meet in the city's local churches on the Friday evening of the Kirchentag. In a festive service, the congregation not only symbolically share food and drink; the format of the service also gives them the opportunity to meet and talk.

For the 3rd Ecumenical Kirchentag it was originally planned to combine the Protestant evening communion service with the Catholic service in such a way that they would take place in parallel on Saturday evening, followed by a joint agape meal after the liturgies. In this way, the confessional services would retain their own character, but would culminate in a subsequent meeting (agape) that would unite the confessions.

The celebration of confessional services on Saturday evening was particularly chosen to comply with the Catholic obligation to go to a Sunday service, a fixed point in the life of believers. In fulfilment of this obligation, whilst making it possible to attend the closing ecumenical service of the ÖKT on Sunday (without having to go to two services), the Evening Mass, which can be held on Saturday evening, forms a legitimate solution of this problem.

Special and specific

All three Ecumenical Kirchentags were charged with the hope of being able to celebrate the Lord's Supper ecumenically, drawing on the Protestant tradition of Holy Communion and the Catholic tradition of the Eucharist. But this hope was not to be fulfilled.

Nevertheless, the first Ecumenical Kirchentag in Berlin in 2003 sent out a strong signal with the joint commemoration of baptism in the opening service, which united the confessions. The second Ecumenical Kirchentag in Munich 2010 sent out a further ecumenical signal by celebrating the Orthodox Artoklasia – breaking of bread – at 1,000 tables on the Odeonsplatz square.

Now the third ÖKT produced a special symbol in the celebration of the Holy Communion and the Eucharist: the denominational services on Saturday evening with an ecumenically sensitive liturgical format.

Denominational, yet ecumenically sensitive

The basis for this particular emphasis was the above-mentioned publication of the Ecumenical Working Group of Protestant and Catholic Theologians (ÖAK) entitled "Together at the Lord's Table".

Particular ecumenical sensitivity is expressed in the mandatory nature of baptism as a prerequisite for participation, by insisting on the use of the term sacrifice in the liturgical language, in the worthy handling of the gifts at the meal, the choosing of ecumenical hymns, the authorisation of the person presiding at the table, the broad participation of all the baptised in the liturgy, as well as in the consideration of the "lay chalice".

The wide open doors

On the Saturday evening of the 3rd ÖKT, the church doors were wide open in many of the parishes in Frankfurt (Protestant, Catholic, Free Church and Orthodox), inviting people to enter in keeping with the motto of this Kirchentag: "Come and see!"

Many Christians who went in through the open doors found themselves joining together in forms of worship that were still unfamiliar – hearing, speaking, feeling, looking and even smelling (despite the obligation to wear a mask).

Four of these services were streamed live from Frankfurt, offering many people the opportunity to participate in these services from afar and to get to know the liturgies of other denominations in this way. These services were also seen by the media to be one of the central moments of the 3rd ÖKT.

The common testimony

A further step was the Common Witness on the occasion of the 3rd ÖKT, which was formulated in a working group and adopted by the Joint Presidium of the 3rd ÖKT (see chapter 6.2). It expresses the common trust in Christ's promise to be present in the celebration of his meal.

A central sentence of the Common Witness is: "As Christians we experience the presence of Jesus Christ in all places where people gather in his name."

Material booklet for support and motivation

In order to support the churches preparing for the Saturday evening and to explain the ecumenical progress theologically, an ecumenical team of the ÖKT developed the material booklet "Come and see! (John 1:39) – Ecumenically sensitive celebration of the Holy Communion and Eucharist". In addition to ecumenical and theological principles, it contains suggestions for planning denominational communion and Eucharist services in an ecumenically sensitive way.

This booklet helps to spread the idea of the Saturday evening services after and beyond the ÖKT.

"Come and see!" beyond the 3rd Ecumenical Kirchentag

Thanks to this special format for the orders of service, the denominational Eucharist and Holy Communion celebrations on Saturday evening took on a new meaning for the ÖKT. The evening was not to be marked by the separation of the confessions, but rather by the inquisitive encounter with liturgies as yet unknown, permitting people to experience the richness of the diverse Christian traditions.

These services were the special feature of the 3rd ÖKT, which was in itself already special. Its message could not be diminished even by the Covid pandemic, namely to enter together with heart and mind into the mystery of the presence of Jesus Christ and, insofar as compatible with one's own conscience, to come to the Communion or Eucharist table, where only Jesus Christ is the host.

Beyond the 3rd ÖKT, these services have laid the foundation for further ecumenical encounters. Holding "ecumenically sensitive" services means that one can come into contact over and over again with the variety of Christian traditions, according to the motto: "Come and see"!

6.2 Witness of ÖKT 3

The Presidium of the 3rd Ecumenical Kirchentag (3rd ÖKT) has formulated and adopted a common witness as part of the preparations for the 3rd ÖKT, which took place in Frankfurt am Main from 12-16 May 2021.

The Presidium was composed of 43 women and men delegated by the organisers, the German Protestant Kirchentag (DEKT) and the Central Committee of German Catholics (ZdK), the host churches and the Council of Churches in Germany (ACK). The Protestant President was Bettina Limperg, the Catholic President Thomas Sternberg.

This common witness unites and strengthens the denominations in their trust in the presence of Jesus Christ in the celebration of the Holy Communion and the Eucharist.

The Common Witness states:

> As Christians, we experience the presence of Jesus Christ in all places where people gather in his name.
> We believe jointly that Jesus Christ himself speaks to us in the proclaimed word of the Gospel.
> We trust that Jesus Christ – as he has promised – is truly and effectively present in the celebration of the Holy Communion and in the celebration of the Eucharist.
> We proclaim his death for us; we believe that he is risen and alive; we hope that he will come again for the salvation of the world.
> Together we celebrate this mystery of our faith and hear his words in remembrance of him: come and see, and recognise me in the breaking of the one bread and in the gift of the one cup for you all. Go out then into the world, transformed and strengthened in my Spirit.
> With the ecumenically sensitive services and this Common Witness, the 3rd Ecumenical Council took a fresh step along the path which is to be continued even more intensively in ecumenical solidarity in the future, taking us further on the way to fulfilling Jesus' request: "May all be one" (Jn 17:21).

7 Denominational liturgical traditions Illustrated by way of example with reference to Sunday, 4 September 2022

7.1 Old Catholic Church (Joachim Pfützner)

1 On the liturgy of Old Catholic eucharistic celebrations in general

In the Old Catholic churches[1] of the Union of Utrecht[2] the Eucharist is celebrated mainly on Sundays and feast days, less frequently on weekdays. If it is possible to hold services on weekdays,[3] these take place mainly in the form of morning or evening praise.[4] Here, as in many other areas, the Old Catholic Churches follow the practice of the early church.[5]

---

[1] The Old Catholic Church is made up of individual autonomous local churches in the sense of the Old Church. Therefore, we can only speak of Old Catholic *Churches*. What follows concerns exclusively the German Old Catholic Church, officially known as: Catholic Diocese of Old Catholics in Germany. See also: Günter Eßer, Die Alt-Katholischen Kirchen (Die Kirchen der Gegenwart 5 – Bensheimer Hefte 116), Göttingen 2016.

[2] Since 1889, the Old Catholic Churches belong as autonomous local churches to the Union of Utrecht. The central body of the Union of Utrecht is the International Old Catholic Bishops' Conference (IBK), whose president is the Archbishop of Utrecht. See Eßer (see note 24), 78-91. Apart from the German Church, the following churches currently belong to the Union of Utrecht: Old Catholic Church in the Netherlands, Christ Catholic Church in Switzerland, Old Catholic Church in Austria, Old Catholic Church in Croatia, Old Catholic Church in the Czech Republic, Polish Catholic Church as well as individual congregations in France and Belgium.

[3] Old Catholic parishes often extend over a larger area, often covering several administrative districts, occasionally even an entire federal state. If only a few parishioners live where the church is situated, it is difficult to celebrate services on weekdays.

[4] With the publication of the currently valid Old Catholic hymnal "Eingestimmt. (1st edition published: Bonn 2003), the so-called "cathedral office" was introduced into

The celebration of the Eucharist is also oriented in many ways towards the practice of the early church. Although the form is hardly any different to that of the Roman Catholic sister church, the Old Catholics had already established it almost a hundred years earlier.[6] The reason is that the first synod of the German diocese, which was founded in 1873, considered it "desirable" to use "the vernacular as the liturgical language in public worship[7] and at the administration of the sacraments".[8] However, it was also explained in the same context that such a reform could only be carried out slowly and gradually, because the necessary liturgical texts would have to be prepared very diligently and thoroughly scrutinised.[9] Thus the second synod called for appropriate scientific discussions by "qualified men" with regard to "the origin and development of the present Western Mass liturgy as a basis for its future reform".[10] And the synod intimated its interest in a "more direct involvement of the congregation".[11] After the completion of this process, a liturgical prayer book for the congregation in the German language was published[12] and three years later an altar book in German for the Eucharist[13]. This already indicated that the liturgy should no longer

---

parish life for the first time in the history of the German Old Catholic diocese. These are forms of Liturgy of the Hours which were developed especially in congregations, and differ from the daily office of monasteries. Cf. Thaddäus A. Schnitker, Morgen- und Abendlob. Prolegomena zu einer aus dem Geist der Alten Kirche erneuerten Tagzeitenliturgie, in: Christus Spes. Liturgie und Glaube im ökumenischen Kontext. Festschrift dedicated to Bishop Sigisbert Kraft, with contributions by Paul Berbers and Thaddäus A. Schnitker ed. by Angela Berlis and Klaus-Dieter Gerth, Frankfurt am Main et al. 1994, 265-275.

[5] Cf. Eßer (as note 50), 21-25.
[6] Cf. Joachim Pfützner, Von der lateinischen zur deutschen Liturgie. Die hart erkämpfte erste Liturgiereform des deutschen alt-katholischen Bistums im Lichte des Münchener Programms, in: Alt-Katholische und Ökumenische Theologie 6 (2021), Bonn 2021, 63-83.
[7] In the 19th century, the term "public worship" meant the Sunday celebration of the Eucharist,
[8] Resolutions of the First Synod of Old Catholics of the German Empire, held at Bonn on 27, 28 und 29 May 1874, official edition, Bonn 1874, 56.
[9] Ibid.
[10] Resolutions of the Second Synod of Old Catholics of the German Empire, held at Bonn on 19, 20 and 21 May 1875, official edition, Bonn 1875, 14.
[11] Ibid.
[12] Liturgisches Gebetbuch. Nebst einem Liederbuche als Anhang, Mannheim 1885.
[13] Das heilige Amt auf die Feste und Zeiten des Jahres, Bonn 1888.

be held by the priest alone, but by the congregation under his leadership. In addition to the priest, a deacon was to participate if possible.[14] There was also provision for other ministries such as a "lector"[15] and a choir[16]; the latter could also be replaced by a cantor[17]. This meant that church music was no longer seen as an accessory embellishing the service, but had become an integral part.[18] This is also evidenced by the publication of a "Book for Choir and Cantor for the Accompaniment of the Songs in the Liturgical Prayer Books".[19] In addition, there were corresponding notes in the liturgical prayer book and the altar book to ensure the participation of the congregation;[20] an entirely choral celebration of the Eucharist in which the congregation could only be listeners had thus become a no-go.[21]

Some of the acclamations which German Old Catholics still use today date back to the first Old Catholic altar book. They respond to the readings of the first part of the Eucharistic celebration, the Liturgy of the Word, with the words: "Thanks be to God, the Lord".[22] After the salutation of peace, exchanged either after the intercessions or before communion, the congregation says, "Peace be with us all!"[23] At the second part of the eucharistic celebration, the liturgy of the Holy Communion, the response

---

[14] The information is given in both the liturgical prayer book and the altar book. For the sake of simplicity, reference is made here only to the altar book (see note 62), here pp. 21, 22, 29. The participation of a deacon, however, remained a theoretical requirement until the 1970s. A permanent diaconate, as is taken for granted today in the Old Catholic Churches, did not exist in the time before, nor did the practice of ordination to the priestly ministry at least one year after ordination to the diaconal ministry.

[15] op. cit., 22.

[16] op. cit., 21, 32.

[17] op. cit., 32.

[18] On the participation of the congregation through the liturgical chants, see: Joachim Pfützner, Adolf Thürling' Liturgisches Gebetbuch und seine Gesänge, in: Internationale Kirchliche Zeitschrift (IKZ) 110 (2020), 148-169.

[19] Chor- und Vorsängerbuch zu den Gesängen des liturgischen Gebetbuchs für die altkatholischen Gemeinden des Deutschen Reiches, Bonn 1890.

[20] Altar book 1888 (see note 62), 32.

[21] However, it took a long time for this to become established in practice. Cf. Sigisbert Kraft, Grundsätze und Ziele altkatholischer Liturgiereform, in: id. Danksagung. Gesammelte Aufsätze zur Liturgie, ed. by Matthias Ring and Florian Groß, Bonn 2015, 9-29, here 20.

[22] Altar Book 1888 (see note 62), 22.

[23] Cf. op. cit., 29.

to the invitation to pray at the offertory is the acclamation "To his glory and for the salvation of the world."[24] "Go forth in peace" at the end of the celebration is followed by the cry "Praise and thanks be to our God!"[25] After the liturgical reform of the Second Vatican Council, these acclamations could certainly have been brought into alignment, just as the German Old Catholic diocese decided at that time to adopt the Roman Catholic lectionary to a large extent, but at that time those responsible for the liturgy considered it more important to preserve the memory of the first liturgical reform, which amounted to a real pioneering effort in translating the texts of the old Missale Romanum into German.

Finally, the form of the Eucharist prayer is also oriented towards examples from the early church[26]. At the 20th International Old Catholic Theological Conference in Altenberg near Cologne in 1979, which dealt with the theology of the Eucharist prayer, a so-called "consensus" was adopted in which it was agreed at the level of the Union of Utrecht to follow the structure of the Early Church Prex Eucharistica when formulating new eucharistic prayers.[27] The clearest feature of this structure, which is found in two variants, is the request for the Holy Spirit to be sent upon the gifts of bread and wine.[28] This takes place after the so-called institution narrative, which ends with the command "Do this in remembrance of me". This command is then put into practice in the so-called anamnesis, the memo-

---

[24] Cf. op. cit. 22. This is preceded by the call of the president: "Pray, beloved, that our sacrifice may be acceptable to the Father, Almighty God. The wording of the congregation's response is, however, slightly changed in the altar book of 1888; it reads "So be it to the glory of his name and the salvation of the world", to which the priest responds with "Amen".

[25] Cf. op. cit., 30.

[26] The German Old Catholic diocese officially introduced the term "Eucharist Prayer" (from Prex Eucharistica) for the prayer that was called "Eucharistic Prayer" in the Roman Catholic Church after the Second Vatican Council; it is borrowed from Old Church usage. See Kraft, Gratiarum actio. Überlegungen zur gegenwärtigen ökumenischen Problematik der Eucharistiefeier, in: id., Danksagung (see note 70), 197-205.

[27] Consensus of the International Old Catholic Theological Conference Altenberg near Cologne 24-28 September 1979, in: IKZ 70 (1980), 226-229. Cf. also the papers presented at the conference, loc. cit. 139-225.

[28] The technical term for this request is "epiclesis" or, more accurately, "epiclesis of the Spirit".

rial of Jesus' death and resurrection.[29] According to the Early Church Prex Eucharistica, this takes place in the simultaneous offering of bread and wine.[30] The goal of this offering is ultimately the request for sanctification of the gifts. However, the Early Church epiclesis extends this request further to all who receive the gifts at communion; they too are to be filled with the Holy Spirit and led to unity. The second variant of Early Church eucharistic prayers includes an additional request for the blessing of the gifts, which already takes place before the institution narrative; however, that makes no difference to the structure after the institution narrative described above. This additional blessing has a specific character of its own – as is expressly emphasised in the "consensus" – and therefore does not replace the epiclesic prayer for the gifts and communicants after the anamnesis.[31]

For Old Catholics, this was an unfamiliar structure after centuries of using the so-called "Canon Romanus", the only eucharistic prayer used in the Roman liturgy, which was also the only eucharistic prayer in Old Catholic churches until the 1970s. For the Canon Romanus also contains a prayer of blessing for the gifts of bread and wine immediately before the institution narrative. Old Catholic theologians had expanded this in the course of the first liturgical reform in the 19th century into an epiclesis of the Spirit.[32] In order to avoid duplication, however, they had altered the recognisably epiclesic invocation for the gifts and communicants after the anamnesis

---

[29] The anamnesis varies in the eucharistic prayers. It is not always limited to the memory of the death and resurrection of Jesus Christ. Often his ascension or exaltation to the right hand of God as well as the prospect of his return are also included in the remembrance.

[30] This is clear from the Latin wording of the oldest complete eucharistic prayer available to us; it is a text from the church order "Traditio Apostolica" (beginning of the 3rd century). The passage reads: "Memores igitur mortis et resurrectionis eius, offerimus tibi panem et calicem ... – In memory of his death and resurrection we offer you the bread and the cup [of wine] ... ".

[31] Consensus (see note 76), 227.

[32] Altar book 1888 (see note 62), 27: "Send us then, we humbly beseech thee, thy Holy Spirit, the giver of all life and sanctification, and let these gifts of the earth be consecrated into heavenly, transfigured, spiritual offerings: that the bread which we break may be the fellowship of the Lord's body, and the cup which we bless the fellowship of the blood of Jesus Christ." See: Kraft, Die Erneuerung der Liturgie in den altkatholischen und anglikanischen Kirchen, in: id., Danksagung (see note 70), 71-84, here 72-74.

by deleting the prayer for the gifts and retaining only the prayer for the communicants.[33] Since the structure of the Early Church Prex Eucharistica had hardly been researched in the late 19th century, the Old Catholic theologians were not aware that their alterations had paved the way for a so-called "divided epiclesis", consisting of a request before the institution narrative relating to the gifts and another after the anamnesis relating to the communicants.[34] For it was precisely this understanding that was to prevail in the Roman Catholic Church – and not only there – in the years after the Second Vatican Council.[35] The Eucharist Book currently used by the German Old Catholic Church also contains a number of prayers with a divided epiclesis, despite the agreements reached in the "consensus".[36] However, the Liturgical Commission decided some years ago that new eucharistic prayers should be composed exclusively according to Early Church structures and that only such prayers should be included in a new Eucharistic Book.

The decision in favour of Early Church structures for the eucharistic prayer also leads to spiritual consequences.[37] For example, the view that the consecration of the gifts of bread and wine takes place at a certain moment of prayer – until the ninth century, it was accepted that Jesus' words "Take, eat, this is my body which is given for you" and "Take, drink, this is the cup of ... my blood which is shed for you" were to be understood as words of consecration – was alien to the ancient Church. This is why they continued to speak of "panem et calicem", of the bread and the chalice, after the institution narrative, while the Canon Romanus speaks of "Panem

---

[33] Op. cit. 28: "In humility we beseech thee, almighty God: that all of us who take part in this communion of the altar and receive thy Son's most holy body and blood may be filled with heavenly blessing and grace".

[34] See on this: Kraft, Die eucharistische Epiklese als ökumenisches Problem. Ein Gesprächsbeitrag, in: id., Danksagung (see note 70), 179-185.

[35] Kraft, Gratias Agamus. Neuere Eucharistiegebete in der ökumenischen Christenheit und die altkirchliche Prex Eucharistica, in: id., Danksagung (see note 70), 141-176, here 153-156.

[36] Die Feier der Eucharistie im Katholischen Bistum der Alt-Katholiken in Deutschland. Für den gottesdienstlichen Gebrauch erarbeitet durch die Liturgische Kommission und herausgegeben durch Bischof und Synodalvertretung, Bonn ³2006, 98-301; 302-305; 306-309; 10-315; 332-335; 336-339.

[37] Herwig Aldenhoven, Die spirituell-theologischen Konsequenzen der Struktur des Eucharistiegebetes, in: IKZ 70 (1980), 212-225.

sanctum vitae aeternae et Calicem salutis perpetuae", the holy bread of eternal life and the chalice of perpetual salvation. Old Catholics today assume that the whole Eucharist prayer has a consecratory character, not just the so-called "words of consecration".[38] But this also gives the instution narrative a different character. It is no longer the centre of the eucharistic prayer, as in the Canon Romanus, but, as in the eucharistic prayer of the Traditio Apostolica, part of the thanksgiving which stands at the beginning of the prayer and which also gives the prayer its name. The ringing of bells, incense and genuflection as Jesus' words are spoken are not customary in the Old Catholic churches, and other gestures such as the elevation of the elements after the respective words of Jesus are also increasingly bing left out.[39] Thus the only gestures that remain are the hands being held over the gifts during the epiclesis and the raising of the gifts during the doxology at the end of the prayer, finally followed by the genuflection of the priest.

Speaking of priests: in the nineties of the 20th century, most Old Catholic Churches of the Union of Utrecht decided to admit women to the priestly and episcopal ministry; women had already been admitted to the ministry as deacons at the beginning of the eighties. In order to avoid complicated gender-inclusive terminology in the German-language eucharistic prayers with intercessions for the Church, it was decided to use the expression "all women and men in apostolic ministry".[40]

Since the 1960s, communion has taken place in both forms; the communicants can choose to drink from the chalice or dip the host into the chalice.[41] There is a so-called eucharistic hospitality, i.e. all baptised persons "who share our faith in the reality and bodily presence of the exalted Lord in the holy sacrament of the altar"[42] are invited to communion. In the German Old Catholic Church this applies in particular to the Evangelical Church in Germany (EKD) due to an "agreement on a mutual invitation to

---

[38] Kraft, Gratias Agamus (see note 84), 146.
[39] Very informative in this regard is: Andreas Krebs, Beziehungsstifter. Zum alt-katholischen Priesterinnen- und Pfarrerinnenbild, in: Alt-Katholische und Ökumenische Theologie 5 (2020), Bonn 2020, 49-62.
[40] Thaddäus A. Schnitker, Die Feier der Eucharistie. Das neue altkatholische Eucharistie-Buch in Deutschland, in: IKZ 86 (1996), 140-146, here 146.
[41] This comes from a decree published in the Official Church Gazette (Amtsblatt) of the Catholic Diocese of Old Catholics in Germany, Vol. XII, No. 10, 13.5.1963.
[42] Official Church Gazette (Amtsblatt) 1971, No. 2, item 3.

participate in the celebration of the Eucharist".[43] If possible, communion takes place in one or more communion groups, which are only dismissed when everyone in the group has received the sacrament.

2 On the liturgy for 4 September 2022, 23rd Sunday of series of readings C

As mentioned above, the German Old Catholic Church has largely adopted the lectionary of its Roman Catholic sister church. This also applies to the numbering of Sundays outside the two festive seasons of Christmas and Easter. The Eucharist Book provides four daily collects for each Sunday of the series of readings, three of them assigned to the series A-C and one to be chosen freely; the latter is a contemporary transcription of the corresponding prayer from the new Missale Romanum. For the 23rd Sunday of the series for year C, this means that one may choose between the collect intended for year C or the one headed "Optional".[44] The content of the prayer for year C is based on the first reading (Wis 9:13-19).[45]

For reading series C, 1st reading:	**Optional:**
Holy God,	Holy God,
your greatness surpasses all our understanding.	you have adopted us as your beloved children.
Free us from presumption, from selfishness and from the burden of our cares,	Look on all who trust in you. Strengthen us in the faith and love and give us a share in your life.
that we may be free to know the inexhaustible riches of your wisdom through our Lord and Master Jesus Christ, who in the unity of the Holy Spirit lives and works with you, now and for ever.	We ask this through Jesus Christ, your Son, our Lord, who in the unity of the Holy Spirit lives and works with you, now and for ever.

---

[43] The text of the agreement can be found in: https://www.kirchenrecht-nordkirche.de/document/40962.
[44] Die Feier der Eucharistie (see note 85), 464f.
[45] op. cit., 465.

A pentitential act at the beginning of the Eucharist is not customary in the German Old Catholic Church. If it is, it should precede the celebration of the Eucharist.[46] The Kyrie chants are therefore basically understood as homage; a prayer for forgiveness between Kyrie chant and Gloria is considered inadmissible. The opening part of the Eucharist constitutes the worshippers as a community of those who belong to Christ[47]; the baptismal formula spoken by the priest is confirmed by the congregation with an "Amen". One element of this constitution is the assurance that they have gathered in the presence of Jesus Christ; this takes place with the liturgical greeting "The Lord be with you!", to which the congregation responds: "And with your spirit." The ensuing Kyrie chants and the Gloria express praise to the Lord who is present in the gathering, and thus also praise of God. This act of constitution comes to an end with the daily collect, preceded by the silent prayers of each member of the congregation.

The Liturgy of the Word basically includes the reading of four biblical texts,[48] the second of which is always a psalm or psalm-like text, which is chanted if possible, and to which the congregation brings a repeated response. The homily is intended to interpret one or possibly several of the biblical texts in relation to the life situation of those assembled. The classic response to the Word of God is first and foremost the intercessions, which on Sundays and feast days are preceded by the creed and can be followed by the greeting of peace. There are no official books or drafts for the intercessions; they should be modelled on the Good Friday intercessions[49], i.e. a succession of prayers for the church, those in government, people in need and the congregation. After each petition there should be a time for silent prayer, which ends with a congregational response. The intercessions should relate to current concerns and are therefore to be freely formulated by the minister or by others commissioned to do so.[50] The Creed is to be understood as a form of baptismal remembrance; either the Apostles' or the

---

[46] op. cit., 181.
[47] This is the meaning of the word "church".
[48] On the 23rd Sunday of reading series C these are: Wis 9:13-19 / Ps 90:3-4, 5-6, 12-13, 14 and 17 / Phlm 9b-10, 12-17 / Lk 14:25-33.
[49] The Good Friday intercessions, which originated in the Roman liturgy, are still considered a structural model for the intercessory prayer today and can be found in: Die Feier der Eucharistie (see note 85), 80-84.
[50] op. cit., 191.

Niceno-Constantinopolitan Creed may be spoken.[51] In the latter case, the "filioque" is omitted, since it does not correspond to the original form of the Creed as established by the general councils of the undivided Church.[52]

The liturgy of the Holy Communion is derived from the biblical tradition of the Last Supper.[53] According to this, the preparation is followed by the eucharistic prayer, the breaking of bread and communion. The preparation, which includes the preparation of the altar, the gifts and the worshippers, should be carried out in a simple form and with the participation of the congregation. The gifts, which include the money taken at the collection beforehand, are brought from the church up to the altar, if possible, by representatives of the congregation and placed there for the eucharistia, the thanksgiving, and the communion that follows. The oblation only takes place as part of the eucharistic prayer; therefore no gestures of offering are made during the preparation. The offertory prayer may be introduced with dialogues between the president and the congregation.[54]

Prayer over the gifts

Good God,
you have fed your people in the desert with manna
and made water to stream from the rock.
You will feed us as well at the table of your Son.
Accept the gifts which we have prepared for this meal
through Christ, our Lord.[55]

---

[51] op. cit., 189-191.
[52] This is how it was settled at the first Union Conference in Bonn in September 1874, first between Old Catholics and Anglicans and then with the Orthodox representatives from Russia and Greece. Cf: Bericht über die 1874 und 1875 zu Bonn gehaltenen Unions-Conferenzen, ed. by Heinrich Reusch. Reprint of the edition in two volumes of 1874 and 1875, with an introduction by Günter Eßer (Geschichte und Theologie des Altkatholizismus, Schriftenreihe des Alt-Katholischen Seminars der Rheinischen Friedrich-Wilhelms-Universität Bonn, ed. by Angela Berlis, Günter Eßer and Matthias Ring, Reihe A: Quellen, Band 2), Bonn 2002, 8-15; 25-28.
[53] Mt 26:26-29; Mk 14:22-25; Lk 22:15-20; 1 Cor 11:23-26.
[54] Die Feier der Eucharistie (see note 85), 195: "**P** Pray, brothers and sisters, that our gifts may be accepted by God the Father Almighty! – **C** For his glory and the salvation of the world." Or "**P** All things come from you. **C** From your own, we bring our gifts."
[55] op. cit., 466.

For the Eucharistic Prayer, the Eucharist Book has a total of 46 prefaces[56] and 23 prayer texts[57] that follow.[58]. For the Sundays in the series of readings, the General Prefaces are the first to be considered.[59] The preface leads into the Sanctus acclamation of the congregation; for this purpose, there are 22 chants[60] in the hymnal "Eingestimmt", some of which, however, hardly reproduce the Sanctus text, or only very incompletely. Among the prayer texts that follow the Sanctus, there are some that are intended only for specific occasions.[61] This means that there are only fifteen texts to choose from for the 23rd Sunday of this series of readings.

In Old Catholic services, great awareness is laid on the breaking of bread. The Eucharistic Book therefore states: "It is recommended that bread be truly broken for all who partake of the eucharistic meal."[62] The process is accompanied by the singing of the Agnus Dei or a suitable hymn.[63] Incidentally, at the preparation there should be only one bowl on the altar for the hosts and only one chalice of wine. In this way, many should eat from the one bread and drink from the one chalice.[64] If it is necessary to administer the gifts at different places in the church, they should be divided up among other bowls and chalices during the breaking of the bread.[65] This is followed by the Lord's prayer and the invitation to communion. Two variants are provided for this in the Eucharist Book:[66]

---

[56] op. cit., 211-277.
[57] op. cit., 279-380.
[58] Four Eucharistic Prayers have their own preface, which cannot be replaced by other prefaces.
[59] op. cit., 244-251.
[60] Eingestimmt. Gesangbuch des Katholischen Bistums der Alt-Katholiken in Deutschland, 2nd corrected and supplemented edition, Bonn 2015, No. 259-260.
[61] Christmas and Christmas season, Reconciliation and Easter penitential season, Maundy Thursday, Easter and Easter season, children's and family services, commemoration of the dead.
[62] Die Feier der Eucharistie (see note 85), 202.
[63] op. cit., 203.
[64] Cf. 1 Cor 10:17.
[65] Die Feier der Eucharistie (see note 85), 202.
[66] op. cit., 203.

Invitation to Holy Communion:

Presider Let us receive the Body of the Lord and call upon his name.

Congregation Lord, I am not worthy to receive you, but only say a word, and I shall be healed.

P This is the bread of life (and the cup of salvation).

C We, being many, are one body, for we all share in the one bread (and in the one cup).[67]

The eucharistic gifts are distributed with the words "The body of Christ" and "The blood of Christ", to which the communicants each respond with an "Amen".[68] Communion is concluded with the Prayer after Communion.

Prayer after Communion:

Good and faithful God,
in the supper of your Son you always let us share anew
in the life of the world to come. We thank you and pray:
May the Spirit, whom we have received,
keep the hope alive in us
and guide us to works of love,
until you will make your creation complete.[69]

The closing part of the eucharistic celebration essentially comprises the blessing and dismissal. These elements may be preceded by the notices to the congregation. On the 23rd Sunday of the series of readings, the words of the blessing are simply "The almighty God bless you: Father, Son and Holy Spirit.".[70] For feast days, the Eucharistic Book offers formulas of solemn blessing with multiple phrases.[71] The dismissal is to be understood as an invitation to become involved as a Christian in the everyday life of the world.

---

[67] The brackets are additions that are not in the Eucharist book, but are used in some congregations with regard to the communion of the chalice.

[68] Alternatively, the formula is often used: "The body of Christ, bread of life" and "The blood of Christ, cup of salvation".

[69] op. cit., 466.

[70] op. cit., 206.

[71] op. cit., 383-397.

7.2 Anglican Church (Christopher Easthill)

1 Introduction to the Eucharist

For the churches of the Anglican Communion there is no globally valid, uniform guideline for the celebration of the Eucharist. Each ecclesiastical province has its own liturgies for this, which, however, have a strong family resemblance due to their common origin in the Book of Common Prayer of the Church of England from the 16th century. In what follows we refer mainly to the practice of the Episcopal Church, which together with the Church of England is one of the two Anglican member churches represented with congregations in Germany.

The Holy Eucharist is defined as the principal act of Christian worship on the Lord's Day and other major Feasts.[72] All believers are urged to observe Sunday through regular participation in the public worship of the Church.[73]

The active participation of the whole Christian assembly is important. All four "estates" – laity, bishops, priests, deacons – should participate actively in the roles assigned to them.

According to the Catechism of the Episcopal Church, the Eucharist is "the Church's sacrifice of praise and thanksgiving" and also "the way by which the sacrifice of Christ is made present, and in which he unites us to his one offering of himself."[74] Among the benefits we receive in the Eucharist is "the strengthening of our union with Christ and one another."[75]

As a weekly celebration of the resurrection, the Eucharist is both a sign and a means of one's own transformation into and through the presence of God. God becomes present in prayer and in the spoken and interpreted Word of God. In the bread and wine, the risen Christ becomes present. At the end of the service, renewed, nourished and strengthened by the sacrament of the body and blood of Christ, we are sent back into the world to transform it according to God's will.

---

[72] Book of Common Prayer of the Episcopal Church (BCP), p. 13 (Service of the Church). Canon B14 of the Church of England prescribes by analogy that Holy Communion must be celebrated in every church (possibly in only one of the churches in the case of large parishes) on Sunday and other important feasts.
[73] Canon II.1 of the Episcopal Church "Of the Due Celebration of Sundays".
[74] BCP, P. 859.
[75] BCP, P. 860.

The 1979 Book of Common Prayer already contains a number of variations for the celebration of the Eucharist, including a variant in traditional language and special liturgies for feast days, as well as particular versions for occasions such as weddings and funerals. Over the years, additional options have been added, including inclusive language. Family, youth or other special services can be designed for specific target groups with a basic structure.

Ecumenical sensitivity

In Anglican churches, all baptised Christians are invited to receive communion in both forms. The choice of biblical texts is also ecumenical, based on the international ecumenical order of the Revised Common Lectionary with the three-year cycle of years A, B, and C.

When the liturgies were redesigned in the 1970s and 1980s, a variety of ecumenical sources were used, so that the eucharistic prayers used today are also based on early Christian models from various traditions. The basic structures were also harmonised at that time. The eucharistic prayer, called the Great Thanksgiving, begins with the *Sursum corda,* and the Preface is followed by the *Sanctus and Benedictus.* The words of institution are based on the text of 1 Corinthians. The *Anamnesis* follows the words of institution, followed in most cases by the *Epiclesis.* According to Anglican understanding, the entire eucharistic prayer is essential for the consecration of the elements.

On ecumenical occasions, clergy of other denominations are involved in the service whenever possible. They can take over the readings and intercessions, but also the sermon. However, only clergy from churches with which there are agreements on church fellowship can celebrate (or concelebrate). On such occasions, there is a preference for the use of ecumenical hymns.

2 Ministries at the Eucharist

For the celebration of the Eucharist, the whole people of God is assembled for the common praise, thanks and service of God. We acknowledge the following ministries in particular:

Readers

Are responsible for the readings from Old Testament, including the Psalm, and the New Testament. The congregation responds to the announcement with an acclamation of thanksgiving.

Prayer leaders or deacons

Are responsible for the intercessions, known as "Prayers of the People". These can be taken from written forms or freely formulated. Petitions are stipulated for the Universal Church, the nations, the welfare of the world, the concerns of the local community and for the departed. Each intercession is followed by a congregational response.

Eucharistic Ministers

Are adults who prepare the altar together with the priest or deacon and participate in the distribution of the gifts.

Altar servers (Acolytes)

If possible, young people should also be involved in serving at the altar, for example by carrying the processional cross and candles.

Musicians

The choir, organists and possibly other musicians accompany the singing of the congregation, or contribute to the dignified and solemn conduct of the service with so-called anthems (choral compositions).

Clergy

If the bishop is present, he usually is the celebrant, otherwise it is a priest. A deacon reads the Gospel, introduces the confession of sin, prepares the altar for communion, and dismisses the people. If there is no deacon, a priest carries out these parts of the service.

3 The order for celebration of the Eucharist

On Sunday, 4 September 2022, the Eucharist will be celebrated according to the Revised Common Lectionary for the 13th Sunday after Pentecost of the corresponding Year C.

It is obligatory that the Eucharist service includes the following text elements: the Collect of the Day, the Lessons as well as the Gospel, the Sermon, the Creed (Niceno-Constantinopolitanum), the Confession of Sin, the Lord's Prayer and the closing prayer. There are several optional forms for the Eucharistic Prayer.

The opening, the intercessions and the music can be chosen freely or according to the season of the church year.

The Word of God

- Opening/greeting:
  The Celebrant (the bishop if present, otherwise a priest) opens the service with the congregation:
  Blessed be God: Father, Son, and Holy Spirit.
  People: And blessed be his kingdom, now and for ever. Amen.
- Optionally (the Celebrant alone or the whole congregation)
  Almighty God, unto whom all hearts are open, all desires known, and from whom no secrets are hid: Cleanse the thoughts of our hearts by the inspiration of thy Holy Spirit, that we may perfectly love thee, and worthily magnify thy holy Name; through Christ our Lord. *Amen*.
- Gloria:
  A hymn or other song of praise
- The Collect of the Day:
  "Grant us, O Lord, to trust in you with all our hearts; for, as you always resist the proud who confide in their own strength, so you never forsake those who make their boast of your mercy; through Jesus Christ our Lord, who lives and reigns with you and the Holy Spirit, one God, now and for ever. Amen."[76]
- 1st reading:
  Old Testament, Jeremiah 18:1-11 or Deuteronomy 30:15-20 (appointed in the lectionary).
- Response Psalm:
  Ps 139, 1-5, 12-17 or Psalm 1 (appointed in the lectionary).
- 2nd reading:
  New Testament, Philemon 1-21 (appointed in the lectionary).
- Gospel:

---

[76] Collect prayer for Proprium 18. p. 233 in the Book of Common Prayer.

Luke 14:25-33 (appointed in the lectionary).
- Sermon:
The sermon interprets one or more of the scripture readings, with particular attention to the needs of the hearers and, where appropriate, the current situation of the world, church or parish.
- The Creed (Niceno-Constantinopolitanum):
Common confession of the Christian faith, on ecumenical occasions without *filioque*.
- Prayers of the People:
Intercessions for the Universal Church, the welfare of the world, the concerns of the local community and for the departed. During Creation Time (1.9. – 4.10) there is often special reference to the theme of creation.
- Confession of Sin:
Joint confession of personal sin in the face of God followed by absolution by the celebrant.
- The Peace:
In words and gestures, the worshippers ask God for peace and exchange a visible sign of reconciliation and unity with each other.

Holy Communion

- The Offertory:
The altar is prepared with the gifts of bread and wine.
- The Great Thanksgiving:
The Eucharistic Prayer. There are several variants to choose from, but some are more appropriate for high feasts or particular seasons. The whole congregation speaks (or sings) the Sanctus and Benedictus, Mystery of Faith and the Great Amen.
- Lord's Prayer:
The Lord's Prayer bonds us together and expresses our unity with one another in Christ. The petition "Give us today our daily bread" is also preparation for receiving communion.
- The Breaking of the Bread:
The bread is broken in silence, followed by the *confractorium* such as "Christ our Passover is sacrificed for us; All: Therefore let us keep the feast."

Often the *Agnus Dei* is spoken or sung as an additional acclamation to the breaking of the bread.
- Communion:
The congregation is invited to communion with the words: "The Gifts of God for the People of God". The bread and cup are distributed with the following words: "The Body of Christ, the bread of heaven. The Blood of Christ, the cup of salvation." The communicant responds in each case with the acclamation Amen.
- Prayer after Communion:
"Eternal God, heavenly Father,
you have graciously accepted us as living members
of your Son our Saviour Jesus Christ,
and you have fed us with spiritual food
in the Sacrament of his Body and Blood.
Send us now into the world in peace,
and grant us strength and courage
to love and serve you
with gladness and singleness of heart;
through Christ our Lord. Amen."[77]
- Blessing[78]:
The celebrant says: "The blessing of God Almighty, the Father, the Son, and the Holy Spirit, be upon you and remain with you for ever. Amen."[79]
- Dismissal:
The deacon or the celebrant dismisses the people, for example with the words "Go in peace to love and serve the Lord"[80], and the congregation responds with "Thanks be to God," in order to go out and live renewed and strengthened as Christians in the world and witnesses to the Gospel.

---

[77] Most frequently used. Alternative prayers are available.
[78] Actually optional, since receiving communion is already "blessing enough," but rarely omitted.
[79] Form is not prescribed, usually trinitarian.
[80] A total of 4 options for dismissal.

7.3 Armenian Apostolic Church (Hacik Gazer)

Die Liturgy of the Armenian Apostolic Church[81]

Sunday, 4 September 2022, is the Third Sunday after the Assumption of Mary, the Mother of God, into Heaven and the beginning of the fasting period before the Feast of the Exaltation of the Cross.

1 Introduction to the Armenian liturgy

Jesus' Last Supper with his disciples forms the centre of Christian worship, according to the Armenian Apostolic Church. The liturgy celebrated today is called "Surp Patarag" (Holy Sacrifice) and is found in the liturgical book "Pataragamatoyc"/"Pataragamatoyc" (Book of Sacrifice, Book of Mystery).[82] The principal part of the liturgical order is ascribed to the Armenian Church Father Gregory the Illuminator (240-326). Until the invention of the Armenian script at the turn of the 4th to 5th century, Aramaic and Greek were used as the languages of worship in Armenia. At that time, depending on the respective sphere of influence, the liturgy of St James from Jerusalem found its way into Armenia via Antioch, while the liturgies of St Chrysostom and St Basil came in via Cappadocia. Thus, the Armenian liturgy can be classified within the Eastern liturgies as a part of the Antiochian branch or family of liturgies. After the invention of the Armenian alphabet, it was then possible to compose prayers and hymns in that language from the 5th century onwards. This development continued until the

---

[81] **Faithful:** approx. 9 million, of whom almost two thirds are in the worldwide diaspora; **Mother See:** Holy Echmiadzin (Armenia); **Head**: Karekin II, Supreme Patriarch and Catholicos of All Armenians; **Dioceses:** 42 dioceses in the Catholicosate of Echmiadzin (9 in Armenia, 15 in Europe, 7 in America, 3 each in Africa and the Middle East, 4 in the Far East and 1 in Australia); 10 dioceses, 3 prelacies and 1 vicariate in the Catholicosate of Cilicia; the Patriarchate of Jerusalem and the Patriarchate of Constantinople; **Liturgical language:** Grabar (Old Armenian); **calendar:** Gregorian (in the Armenian Patriarchate of Jerusalem: Julian).

[82] The Armenian word Patarag (sacrifice) is equivalent to the Greek word Anaphora. The Armenian word patarag has many gradations and variety of meanings. It can mean: 1. Tusia: hostia, sacrificium; 2. Prosphora: oblatio; 3. Doron: donum, munus; 4. Leiturgia/Ierourgia: liturgia, missa, sacrificium. In the context of the celebration of the meal, the word patarag denotes on the one hand the gifts offered and on the other hand also the act of offering.

17th century, when the first liturgical books were printed. In addition, the Latin Mass was translated into Armenian in the Middle Ages and parts of it, such as the "Prayers at the Foot of the Altar" in the opening section of the Latin Mass, which were removed from the Latin Mass after Vatican II, are preserved and prayed in the Armenian liturgy to this day. To sum up, it can be said that the Armenian liturgy as it is used today has become an extremely original synthesis, consisting of parts of Armenia's own liturgical texts dating back to the 5th century alongside liturgical elements from the sister churches.

There are two Armenian composers who set the Armenian liturgy to music in the Western notation in the late 19th and early 20th centuries, namely Makar Jekmaljan (1856-1905) and Komitas Vardapet Soghomonian (1869-1935). Nowadays, versions of the liturgy composed by these two church musicians are sung and prayed with the accompaniment of the organ, which was not introduced in the Armenian Church until the 19th century.

In view of this liturgical tradition, it should be clear that today the members of other churches and denominations, who are baptised members of their own churches, can not only participate in the celebration of the Armenian liturgy, but are also invited to communion. However, the "official" church communion only exists between the members of the Armenian Church and those of the four other Oriental churches (Ethiopian, Coptic, Syriac, and some of the Saint Thomas Christian churches).

2 Ministries before, during and after the Armenian liturgy

Parishioners and those officiating (priests, deacons, choirmasters) prepare for the liturgical celebration, which can usually be held on every Sunday and feast day, as well as on saints' or martyrs' days during the week. Fasting, prayer and confession may be part of the preparation for the liturgical celebration. Confession can be made individually or as a general confession during the liturgical celebration. In the latter case, the deacon reads a catalogue of vices on behalf of the congregation, to which the parishioners respond with the words "I have sinned and I repent".

The host, known in Armenian as "nshkhar", is the small bread for the eucharistic presentation and is usually prepared on the previous evening by the celebrant or deacon. It is a little round loaf of unleavened dough from pure wheat without salt, which is stamped with an image of the cross before being baked.

In addition to this bread/host, Armenians use another bread in the service, the "mahs", which literally means portion and is a very thin unleavened wheat bread. Unlike the host "nshkhar", this bread can be baked by any member of the congregation and used for the celebration. This bread is distributed to the congregation at the end of the liturgy. It is a custom to take some of this bread home to members of the family or neighbours who were unable to come to receive communion. The wine is red wine. Armenians do not dilute the wine with water. For this they were condemned as heretics in the time of the Early Church. Communion is distributed under both kinds. What is left over is used to administer communion to the sick and for other special pastoral uses.

3 Order of the Armenian liturgy

The basic form of all the liturgies is derived from the service of the word at the synagogue and the prayers of thanksgiving at the Jewish meal. From these two elements, the four sections of the Armenian liturgy were developed:

1. The service of preparation
2. The service of the word
3. The service of sacrifice
4. The blessing and dismissal

The service of preparation/opening
The first section consists of four parts: the robing, the washing of hands and confession of sins by the celebrant, the ascending of the altar steps in front of the congregation, and the preparation of the wine and bread for the celebration of the meal.

While the hymn is sung *"O deep mystery"* (by Khachatur of Taron, 13th century), the celebrant, accompanied by the deacons, comes out of the vestry and approaches the altar. He washes his hands and, in turns with a deacon, recites Psalm 26. After that, they recite Psalm 100: "Make a joyful noise to the Lord, all the earth. Serve the Lord with gladness: come before his presence with singing!" and Psalm 43 "Then will I go to the altar of

God, to God my exceeding joy". During these readings, the celebrant and deacon ascend the altar steps together.

In the Armenian church there is no iconostasis between the nave of the church and the sanctuary or bema, but there is a curtain. Several times during the service, the curtain in front of the altar is drawn, and the celebrant reads prayers, some of them quietly and some aloud, often behind the drawn altar curtain. The curtain is closed while the bread and wine are being prepared, then it is opened, and there is a solemn procession before the proper service of the word begins.

Service of the word
It is now time to listen attentively to the biblical truths. The Old Testament and New Testament lessons are read which are appointed according to the topic or commemoration of the day.

On this Sunday, 4 September 2022, the following readings are stipulated:
Old Testament: Book of the Prophet Isaiah 10:12-19
A lamentation and a proclamation of judgment against proud Assyria
New Testament: 2 Corinthians 2:12-3:3
The proclamation of the gospel as Christ's triumphal procession and the glory of service to the new covenant
Gospel: Mark 6, 30-44
The Feeding of the Five Thousand

This is followed by the recital of the Creed as the congregation's response to the Gospel.

In the Old Church, the sermon was now preached, followed by the dismissal. Today, the sermon is preached either before or after the distribution of the gifts of bread and wine, i.e. the communion.

Traces of the dismissal prayer are still recognisable and are also prayed. With this prayer the catechumens and penitents were asked to leave the nave and follow the rest of the liturgy in the courtyard of the church. For this reason the deacon says at this point: "Let none of the catechumens, none of little faith and none of the penitents or the unclean draw near to this divine mystery, but let them now go outside to continue praying there."

Holy Communion – Service of sacrifice – Anaphora – Eucharistic Prayer – Preface

The Surp Patarag liturgy can be compared to an ellipse with two radiant stars at the focal points: Gospel and Communion. The Eucharistic Prayer is a composition consisting of several parts: Introductory Dialogue, Prayer before the Sanctus, Sanctus, Prayer after the Sanctus, Communion Narrative, Anamnesis, Epiclesis, Anaphoric Intercession and Doxology.

It starts with the great entrance procession, accompanied by the recitation of Psalm 24:7: "Lift up your gates, O princes; let the everlasting doors be lifted up, and the king of glory shall come in." Then the deacon lifts up the wine and the bread (chalice and paten) and carries them up to the celebrant. After the priest asks "Who is the king of glory?" (Psalm 24:8), the wine and bread are transferred by the deacon to the priest with the words "This is the king of glory!" (Psalm 24:10).

This part of the service is immediately followed by the Kiss of Peace.

Since the Lord has arrived and is present at the holy table in the form of bread and wine, that is sufficient reason to exchange the Kiss of Peace before the words of institution and the epiclesis. The deacon invites the faithful to exchange the Kiss of Peace. While the choir sings the hymn "Christ in our midst has been revealed", the deacon descends from the sanctuary and exchanges the kiss with other clergy who are present, with ecumenical guests and with the members of the congregation. The faithful pass on the Kiss of Peace to each other until all have received the holy greeting from the holy table. The one who offers the kiss says: "Christ is revealed among us." The response is, "Blessed is the revelation of Christ."

Inspired by the mutual Kiss of Peace, the faithful join the heavenly seraphim and cherubim in chanting the Sanctus "Holy, holy, holy, Lord of hosts".

Now follows the Eucharistic Prayer. The introduction is a Trinitarian Benediction. The Creator is thanked for his work of salvation, for his mercy and the redemptive work of Christ. This is followed by the anamnesis, recalling the great deeds of redemption, Christ's suffering, crucifixion, death and burial, his resurrection on the third day and ascension and the events of Pentecost. After this come the words of institution and the epiclesis. The prayers for the deceased and for the living encompass both Armenian and non-Armenian saints and martyrs and all who confess Christ from the whole church in all the world. This is followed by the Lord's Prayer. During the subsequent prayer of inclination, the congregation bows down and kneels, while the gifts are raised in the Elevation, i.e. in veneration.

The bread is broken into three parts and dipped into the wine. The violent death and resurrection of Jesus Christ, by which the sins of the world were taken away, are made visible here. First the priest himself receives the communion, then the members of the congregation approach the altar and receive the Holy Meal under both forms. During the distribution, it is not the faithful who kneel, but the priest.

After the communicant has received the host, it should not be chewed, but swallowed whole. At the end of the liturgy, the Armenian Church distributes the blessed bread "mahs" for those who, for whatever reason, were not able to partake of the Holy Communion. This is probably an ancient Christian custom, reminiscent of the love feast (agape) of the early Christian community. The custom of distributing blessed bread (gr. antidoron, arm. mas) is also characteristic of other Orthodox churches.

Conclusion: Thanksgiving and Dismissal

After the distribution, the altar curtain is drawn. The celebrant collects the remnants of the host, cleans and dries the chalice, while quietly saying a prayer of thanksgiving. *"We have been filled with your good things, O Lord, by tasting of your Body and Blood. Glory in the highest to you who have fed us... "* and *"We give thanks to you, Lord, who have fed us at your table of immortal life; distributing your Body and your Blood for the salvation of the world and for life to our souls."*

The altar curtain is opened. The celebrant says the prayer of John Chrysostom, *"O Lord, who blesses those who bless you... "*. The celebrant or the most senior clergy member present blesses and dismisses the congregation in peace with the words, *"Be blessed by the grace of the Holy Spirit. Depart in peace and the Lord be with you all. Amen"*.

7.4 Federation of Pentecostal Churches (Frank Uphoff)

Communion celebrations in congregations of the BFP[83]
Taking the example of the Christus Gemeinde Velbert (CGV)

Introduction

Congregations of the BFP celebrate Holy Communion regularly. In many congregations it is celebrated on the first Sunday of the month at the public worship service. Other congregations hold Holy Communion at internal services during the week. On special occasions, such as Maundy Thursday or Good Friday, there is an additional celebration of Holy Communion. Small groups (so-called house groups, ConnectGroups, ...) also hold communion services.

Here we show how the communion is practised in the BFP by taking the Christus Gemeinde Velbert as an example. This church is 114 years old, and therefore the oldest congregation of the BFP; it comprises about 320 baptised members, plus friends, children and young people who have not yet decided to be baptised in faith (by immersion).

Freedom vs. theological reflection on the celebration of the Communion

Basically, the BFP congregations are free to organise their own way of celebrating Holy Communion. There are no fixed liturgical guidelines that must be followed, although the forms of service and expressions used tend to be similar. The service celebration often concentrates strongly on the fellowship character, as the members of free churches often have a strong network of friendships and relationships – especially in the smaller congregations.

The service of Holy Communion has undergone a change in the course of the last decades. Whereas Pentecostal congregations with leaders from

---

[83] The Federation of Pentecostal Churches (BFP) is the second largest free church within the Association of Evangelical Free Chruches (VEF) in Germany. The BFP has 62,872 members in 836 congregations. 325 of them (38.9%) are migration congregations. If children, youth and regular guests are included, approximately 181,255 people belong to the BFP (as of 01.01.2019). Further information at www.bfp.de.

an older generation had developed a form that was more traditionally-minded (communion led by an ordained pastor, usually distributed only by male "church elders", mostly in ties and dark suits, a regular order of service in carefully chosen language, ...), there is nowadays in most cases a more informal structure (both men and women are involved, the dress order is casual and the language colloquial, so that the form and order of service are of secondary importance and the structure can vary greatly. This is also connected to the fact that in the congregations of the BFP the leadership is increasingly in the hands of younger people, or else recently founded churches have started up and adopt unconventional attitudes).

Although on the one hand the BFP welcomes and desires freedom in the structure of the communion service, the meaning of the Holy Communion is well reflected theologically. In 2007, a volume of reflections dedicated to the theme of the Holy Communion was published by the BUW (now FThG, Forum Theologie & Gemeinde).[84]

The practice of Holy Communion is reflected in a book "Kasualien in der Freikirche" (special services in the free church), also published by the FThG[85]. The following section on the significance of Holy Communion is taken from this publication.

Five meanings of Holy Communion

We find four accounts in the New Testament that provide the basis of Holy Communion. All four have in common that they report on the Last Supper which Jesus shared with his disciples on the eve of his death on the cross. Three of them are to be found in the Synoptic Gospels[86], another version by Paul in his letter to the church in Corinth[87]

The various aspects of Holy Communion unfold the fullness of its meaning and indicate its power and promise. In the following, five

---

[84] Das Abendmahl. Published by the Forum Theologie & Gemeinde of the BFP. Erzhausen, 2011

[85] "Für den besonderen Anlass: Kasualien in der Freikirche". Published by the Forum Theologie & Gemeinde of the BFP. Erzhausen, 2011

[86] Mk 14:12-26; Mt 26:17-30; Lk 22:7-23

[87] 1 Cor 11,23-25

meanings are briefly described – each based on a significant biblical passage.

Memory *"Do this in remembrance of me!" (Lk 22:19)*
As we eat the bread and drink from the cup, we look to the cross in faith and marvel at the love of God revealed there. "In remembrance of me" refers first and foremost to the person of Jesus. At the Holy Communion, we are reminded afresh that Jesus loved us to the end (Jn 13:1 – word for word).

Proclamation *"For as often as you eat this bread and drink the cup, you proclaim the Lord's death until he comes." (1Cor 11:26)*
Holy Communion is a preaching service. At Holy Communion we confess all that Jesus has done for us by his death on the cross: perfect redemption and forgiveness from guilt, deliverance from the power of sin – indeed, salvation for body, soul and spirit! But we also proclaim that he will come again ("until he comes"), thus beholding the full extent of his victory. Through his death he has conquered all his enemies and is now seated at the right hand of the Father "far above all rule and authority".[88]

The aspect of proclamation means that Holy Communion has a particular effect on faith, since faith comes from what is heard (Rom 10:17). When we celebrate Holy Communion, we are strengthened in our belief and renewed in our certainty, and that leads to the joy and freedom of faith.

Covenant *"This cup is the new covenant in my blood." (Lk 22:20)*
In Holy Communion we celebrate God's new covenant with humanity, which is no longer characterised by a righteousness through works, but by the righteousness that comes from faith. I must no longer earn my salvation, but am granted it completely undeservedly. In the Holy Communion, however, we not only confess what God has done, but also enter anew into the new covenant with God and affirm our decision for Christ. Whoever receives Holy Communion renews the promise made to God at baptism: "I am buried with Christ and now present my life to God."[89]

---

[88] Eph 1:21
[89] Rom 6:4, 13

Fellowship (Communion) *"The cup of blessing that we bless, is it not a sharing in the blood of Christ? The bread which we break, is it not a sharing in the body of Christ?" (1Cor 10:16)*
Through the Holy Communion we enter into a special fellowship[90] or participation in Christ's body and blood. This speaks of a real presence of Christ in the Holy Communion (but no mystical connection with bread and wine), whereby we can imagine that the relationship between Christ and the elements is similar to the connection between God and the written word (the Bible). God may not be physical in paper and ink, but as I read his Word I receive far more than mere information for my mind; I participate in the very life of God because the Holy Spirit brings the Word to life and connects with it, so to speak. In the same way, I transcend the purely symbolic character of the elements when I believe in what the elements represent: I come into contact with Christ himself.

Unity *"We who are many are one body, for we all partake of the one bread." (1 Cor 10:17).*
Thus the Holy Communion also expresses in a special way the unity of the body of Jesus or the church. Just as at the Passover celebration in the old covenant there was one lamb for one house, so that all the inhabitants of the house gathered around the one lamb and thus also identified with each other, so we too identify with each other at the joint service of Communion. Of course, this presupposes that the participants in the Holy Communion have also personally accepted Christ as Saviour and are not just officially members of a church somewhere.

These are the points taken from the publication mentioned above.

The understanding of Holy Communion at the Christus Gemeinde

In the CGV we emphasise the meanings of the Holy Communion as set out here. For us, the Holy Communion is not merely a "commemorative meal". At Holy Communion Christ is spiritually present. We do not understand the words "This is my body, this is my blood"[91] in the sense of a physical presence of the Lord, but in the sense of a spiritual reality.

---

[90] Literally "koinonia", from which Latin "communio" is derived.
[91] 1 Cor 11:24,25

Participation in Holy Communion

The Christus Gemeinde has always taken participation in Holy Communion very seriously. Minutes of church meetings from the 1930s state that the membership status could be revoked if someone had not "taken part in the breaking of bread for more than a year". Nowadays there is no such restrictive practice, but the spiritual understanding has not fundamentally changed. The importance of (regular) participation in the Holy Communion is emphasised again and again. For elderly members of the congregation who are unable to attend (due to health reasons) Communion can be brought to them at home.

The invitation to participate in the Holy Communion is usually open. It is emphasised that one should "belong to the people of God" on the basis of a personal life commitment to Jesus Christ. Faith baptism (by immersion), which is also emphasised as a sign of such firm commitment, is not compulsory, but warmly recommended. Members of other churches and denominations, or of none, are also invited to come to Communion, as long as they can testify that they are "personally certain" that they belong to the "Church of Jesus Christ" (in the sense of the invisible community).

Reconciled relationships are another important aspect of the Holy Communion service. The Holy Communion is used again and again to refer to mutually clarified relationships and clarification of open issues.

At Holy Communion there is the offer of prayer for the sick (in some cases including the anointing with oil[92]). There have been some astonishing personal reports of healing through such prayer for the sick.

Basically, we emphasise the freedom of the personal decision to take part in Holy Communion, in accordance with the words of the Apostle Paul: "Examine yourselves, and only then eat of the bread and drink of the cup"[93].

During the communion service, children below the age of religious majority usually take part in the children's service (without communion). Should they attend the adults' service, it is up to the parents to decide about their participation at Holy Communion.

---

[92] Cf. Jas 5,16ff
[93] 1 Cor 11:28

The framework of the service of Holy Communion, taking the example of the Christus Gemeinde Velbert

On September 4, 2022, the Christus Gemeinde celebrates Holy Communion at the main morning service at 10 am. On this day there will be another service ("+service") at 7 pm with the focus on the "younger generation", where Holy Communion is only held from time to time, but according to a similar pattern.

Before the service, the Communion is prepared by a special team. Suitable unleavened bread (for example, white toast) is cut into small pieces and prepared on several plates. Several trays hold about 30-40 small communion cups filled with grape juice, sometimes also with wine as an alternative. These are placed on three or four bistro tables in different parts of our large church. Otherwise they are all placed on a single table at the front of the church.

Formerly there was a common chalice from which all the participants drank one after the other, but this is no longer used at the main services of the Christus Gemeinde. There are no theological reasons for this, but only because of the changed attitudes to hygiene.

We send a message in advance to people from the online congregation, who join us via YouTube stream, asking them to get ready for communion by preparing some bread and wine or juice. We repeat this request at the start of the livestream.

When house groups or other small groups celebrate Communion together, they usually take a common chalice and an uncut loaf of bread. In such cases, it is usual to include other informal elements that strengthen the fellowship, for example prayers of blessing and consolation, embracing, prayers for the sick, and so on. It is left to the groups to decide who should lead the communion service. These persons are then prepared for their ministry in special training courses.

The order of the communion service

The communion service in the CGV does not follow a fixed liturgical scheme. Each communion service can therefore have a slightly different character with different emphases.

This is also related to the openness to the charisms[94], for the use of such gifts is basically welcome in the services of the CGV. By prior arrangement, people have the opportunity to pass on spiritual messages, prophetic visions, utterances of wisdom or words of discernment. Since the content cannot (and should not) be planned, this can have a strong influence on the character of a service, and this is usually experienced as very beneficial.

- **Information slides** on the CGV on the video projector and the live stream, displaying a countdown timer
- **Opening of the service** with a song in praise of God by the **worship team**
- **Welcome** of the congregation in church and online by the moderator of the service, possibly reading a bible text of their own choice.
- **Sharing the experience** made by one of the worshippers with "Jesus in everyday life" or another "special" happening. This person, who has been determined in advance, tells of an experience from everyday life which is intended to encourage others. It might also be a report from our foreign workers ("missionaries"), possibly on video. (Duration: up to ten minutes)
- Announcement of the **songs of praise** song by the moderator
- **Worship time:** A time of singing and prayer with several songs, interrupted by prayers as appropriate, from the microphone. Led by a worship team and its leader. The songs have been chosen beforehand. Duration: approx. 15 minutes
- **Sermon** by the pastor of the congregation or a preacher (a guest, or from the ranks of the congregation). As a rule, a **sermon series** is preached over several Sundays. Duration: approx. 30 min
- **Response time** – prayer after the sermon, invitation to personal response, invitation to confess Christ, openness to prophetic gifts (see above) to be reviewed by the pastor / moderator and then shared over the microphone. (5 to 10 minutes)
- **Worship song** or other musical contribution (by the band or soloist)
- **Preparation of Holy Communion:** About six to ten previously selected communion assistants come to the central communion table to the leader of the communion or go directly to the bistro tables with the gifts.

---

[94] Cf. Paul's explanations on this in 1 Cor 12.

- **Introduction** to the Holy Communion by the pastor or the leader of the communion
  - Optional Bible text reading
  - A brief thought on one aspect of the meaning of the Holy Communion (see above).
  - Optional prayer
  - Open invitation to the Holy Communion
  - Optional explanation about taking part in Holy Communion (referring to baptism, possible necessity to clarify relationships, confession of sins, reference to the Prayer lounge).
- **Spontaneous and freely formulated prayer of blessing** for the bread and cups by the communion helpers or the leader of the communion.
- **Alternative methods of distribution:**
  - The worshippers come one by one to the bistro tables where they are handed the bread and the cup with spontaneous words of blessing. These blessings are not fixed and are left up to the communion helper.
  - The communion helpers bring the plate with the bread and the tray with the cups to the worshippers and these are passed through the rows, where each participant helps himself or herself.
  - Due to the Covid pandemic, there may also be alterations to this practice in connection with increased hygiene precautions. (For example, one piece of bread and a small communion cup may be served on a tiny plate covered by a glass dessert bowl).
- The distribution is usually **accompanied and supported musically by** the worship group, which then celebrates Holy Communion for itself after the service.
- **Alternative methods of receiving communion:**
  - All worshippers take the bread and the cup back to their places, where they will receive it, all eating and drinking together. The leader of the communion will explain this and give the appropriate instructions.
  - The worshippers divide into small groups of two or three persons, pray for each other, sharing Bible verses, spiritual promises or personal prophetic messages. Usually there is a special guidance for this.

- o Inclusion of the online congregation in Holy Communion, inviting them to receive it in their own homes, too. (Pictures of the situation in church are shown.)
  - o Conclusion: The empty cups are gathered in by the communion assistants.
- Parallel to the distribution / celebration, a blessing team / prayer team is available in the **"Prayer lounge"**. Worshippers can go there and receive a blessing or be prayed for.
- In some cases, there is the offer of **prayer and anointing with oil** (anointing of the sick) by people delegated to do so.
- Duration of the communion part of the service: approx. 15 minutes, longer if necessary
- **Prayer of thanksgiving,** possibly the **Lord's Prayer** (not common in all cases)
- Sometimes a final **song of praise or confession of faith**
- The moderator **closes the service** with final announcements and the collection appeal, which is not collected in cash due to Covid-19.
- **Prayer of blessing** by the moderator (either pre-formulated or spontaneous, according to preference)
- Closing song

The people involved

Here are the persons who are active at the service in the order mentioned above.

- **Communion preparation team**: One or two people who do the practical preparations for communion.
- **Worship team:** A band consisting of several musicians (usually playing guitar, piano/keyboard, bass, drums) and several singers.
- The **moderator of the service** is a "host" who welcomes the people and guides them through the service as necessary. This is done in a rather minimalist way.
- **Worshippers at the service:** People visiting the service can take part with their spontaneous or previously announced contributions, depending on the framework. The different possibilities are coordinated with them individually.
- **Pastor** – one of the pastors of the church. We currently have two pastors at the Christus Gemeinde, it used to be three. The sermon may

also be preached by another member of the church leadership, or another church member if necessary. There is a preaching schedule.
- **Leader of the Holy Communion**: usually the senior pastor of the congregation or another member of the church leadership. It may also be the moderator of the service.
- **Communion assistants:** members of the congregation who help to distribute Holy Communion, often people who do other church work.
- **Blessing Team / Prayer Team:** Team trained in pastoral care who are available for conversation and prayer.

Final thoughts

At the Christus Gemeinde Velbert, it is most important to celebrate Holy Communion, and the church members and visitors attend the service regularly and gladly.

The church leadership emphasises the importance of the Holy Communion. We consider it particularly important to us to hold the communion service in various forms, with different wording and changing emphases, so that the precious message is always packaged and communicated in a fresh and vivid way.

7.5 Evangelical Churches in the EKD (Julia Meister)

1 Introduction to the celebration of the Lord's Supper

In the Lord's Supper, the Christian community celebrates the new communion with God and with one another opened up by Jesus' saving work. The Evangelical Church shares the ecumenical insight that it is the living Christ himself who invites us to his table and into his fellowship. In worship, the Lord's Supper stands in continuity with the proclaimed Word: it is the salvific address through the gospel of God that re-orientates the human heart in faith and allows us to experience God's covenant with his creation.[95]

---

[95] "As a sacrament, it also conveys nothing other than the proclamation of the Word, but it conveys this in a special way. The proclamation of the biblical Word is complemented by being seen and tasted (the sacrament becomes bodily accessible to certain senses), by a specific connection between individuality and fellowship (the

In the Leuenberg Agreement of 1973, the Lutheran churches laid down a common understanding of the Lord's Supper, establishing communion between Lutheran, Reformed and United churches. Despite all the theological agreements recorded there, the Leuenberg Agreement is at the same time open to interpretation and appropriation by the respective church tradition.

The member churches of the EKD have different traditions as to when and how often the Lord's Supper is celebrated. The decision as to whether the Lord's Supper is celebrated monthly or weekly, for example, is up to the local congregations.

2 Participants in the Protestant Communion service

The service is celebrated by the entire congregation. Apart from the inward participation, e.g., by joining in prayer, there are various forms of participation that individual members of the congregation can perform. These include, for example, the reading of scriptural texts, the intercessory prayers, or the musical accompaniment. Frequently, members of the congregation help to distribute the elements at the communion service. The public proclamation of the Word and the celebration of the Lord's Supper are led by an ordained person. This corresponds to the Protestant understanding, according to which all members of the congregation are qualified by their baptism for priestly service ("priesthood of all believers"), but only certain individuals are commissioned to perform it. The ordained ministry works in to serve the congregation and is commissioned by the congregation.

---

sacrament is administered to individual people in the worshipping community), and by its confessional character (the sacrament must be expressly desired by the individual communicant)." Das Abendmahl. Eine Orientierungshilfe zu Verständnis und Praxis des Abendmahls in der evangelischen Kirche. Presented by the Council of the Evangelical Church in Germany, Gütersloh 20085, 25 (available online at: https://www.ekd.de/ekd_de/ds_doc/abendmahl.pdf.

3 Order of the Holy Communion in the form of the Protestant Mass[96]

The communion service has four parts, which unfold the service as an event of communication between the members of the congregation and with God.

The pericope order of the Evangelical Church in Germany determines the readings appointed for the Sunday service.[97] The texts are selected and combined according to the church year. For each Sunday in the church year, the pericope order includes the readings of the biblical texts, two options for the weekly hymn, a biblical weekly motto, the weekly psalm, and the Hallelujah verse. The binding nature of this lectionary is handled differently in the regional churches. On the First Sunday of Advent 2018, the new pericope order came into force, which, among other things, takes greater account of Old Testament texts. Each Sunday is assigned a theme. Sunday, 4 September 2022, belongs to the season of Trinity that begins after Pentecost and the Feast of Trinity and is said to be "festival-free". The focus is on God's work of creation, reconciliation and consummation in the unity of his Trinity. The liturgical colour of this season is green – the colour of hope and growth. September 4, the 12th Sunday after Trinity, has the theme "Faith in Everyday Life." The readings appointed (see below) remind us that the work of God opens our eyes and ears. God reveals unexpected perspectives and lets us discover things anew in the horizon of his Trinitarian work.

Indispensable elements of the Protestant meal celebration, in addition to the words of institution, are the Lord's Prayer, the distribution of the elements, and a prayer of thanksgiving to God.[98]

---

[96] In the Protestant member churches of the EKD, two forms of worship are common: the Protestant Mass and the Upper German sermon service. Here the Protestant Mass will be presented. A detailed description and explanation of the individual service elements of both liturgies is given in the EKD's orientation guide: "Der Gottesdienst. Eine Orientierungshilfe zu Verständnis und Praxis des Gottesdienstes in der evangelischen Kirche, Im Auftrag des Rates der EKD," 2009, ed. Gütersloher Verlagshaus. Available online at: https://www.ekd.de/der_gottesdienst.htm. The description that follows is derived from Section 4, "Gottesdienst als Gestaltungsaufgabe" (Worship as a Formative Task).

[97] An overview of the church year, all feast days and the pericope order can be found under: https://www.stilkunst.de/index.php

[98] Cf. Das Abendmahl (see note 144), p. 49

A – Opening and invocation

- Ringing of church bells
- Music at the entrance procession
- Greeting
- Hymn
- Salutation
  In the salutation, the assembled congregation and the liturgist greet each other mutually. The invocation of the triune God – "In the name of God, the Father and the Son and the Holy Spirit" – is a recollection of baptism.
- Psalm
  With the psalm, the congregation joins in the prayer of Israel. Using the words of the psalmists, it praises and glorifies God, expresses sorrows and requests, hope and comfort. The congregation and the liturgist, or else two groups of the congregation, speak alternate verses. The weekly psalm for 4 September 2022 is Psalm 147:1-6, 11. The psalm is closed by praise of the Trinity: "Glory be to the Father, and to the Son, and to the Holy Spirit. Amen."
- Lord have mercy (Kyrie)
- Glory to God (Gloria)
- Collect of the Day

B – Proclamation and Confession

- Scripture Reading
  There are three possible scripture readings: the reading from the Old Testament, from the New Testament Epistles, and from the Gospels. For 4 September 2022, the pericope order foresees the following readings: OT reading: Isaiah 29:17-24; Epistle: Acts 9:1-20; Gospel: Mark 7:31-37.
- Hymn
- Sermon text and sermon: the sermon text for 4 September 2022 is Acts 9:1-20.
- Creed
  As a rule, the congregation prays the Apostolic Creed. If the Nicene Creed is said, it is a clear expression by the congregation expresses of its ecumenical bond with other Christian churches.
- Intercessory prayer

C – Communion

- Hymn
  - Thank offering
  - Offertory Prayer
- The celebration of Holy Communion is accompanied by a eucharistic liturgy that begins with the reciprocal greeting of the congregation (Preface), takes up the praise of the Triune God (Sanctus), and concludes with the petition for Christ's peace and mercy ("Christ, Lamb of God").

  - Prayer of Praise (Preface):

    > "The Lord be with you.
    > Congregation: And with your spirit.
    > Lift up your hearts.
    > C   We lift them up unto the Lord.
    > Lct us give thanks to the Lord our God.
    > C   That is worthy and right.
    > It is indeed worthy and right,
    > That we praise you, eternal God, and give you thanks
    > At all times and in all places
    > Through our Lord Jesus Christ.
    > You sent him into the world for our salvation,
    > Through his death we have forgiveness of sin
    > And through his resurrection we have life.
    > Therefore the angels praise your glory,
    > The powers worship you, and the mighty fear you.
    > All the hosts of heaven rejoice in praising you;
    > We join with them in raising our voices
    > And confess without end:"

  - Sanctus

    > C   Holy, holy, holy is God, the Lord of hosts;
    > heaven and earth are full of his glory.
    > Hosanna in the highest.
    > Blessed is he who comes in the name of the Lord.
    > Hosanna in the highest.

- Eucharistic celebration and words of institution

The liturgist addresses the congregation with the words of institution of Jesus according to the biblical accounts of Jesus' last meal with his disciples. The words of institution are the realisation for the congregation that Jesus has promised to be present in the celebration of his meal. In the Protestant tradition, the promise of the words of institution is an indispensable part of the communion liturgy.
- Lord's Prayer
- The Peace greeting: the congregation exchange the peace of God with one another.
  - Lamb of God (Agnus Dei).

    C   Christ, you Lamb of God, that takes away the sins of the world, have mercy upon us.
        Christ, you Lamb of God, that takes away the sins of the world, have mercy upon us.
        Christ, you Lamb of God, that takes away the sins of the world, grant us your peace.

- Distribution
The congregation is invited to the Lord's Table to celebrate with bread and wine. The words of institution heard before make clear: it is Christ himself who invites us! The liturgist introduces the distribution with the words:

"Come, for all is prepared. Taste and see that the Lord is good."
  - Offertory words:
    "Take and eat:
    The Body of Christ, who died for your sins.
    Take and drink:
    The Blood of Christ, shed for your sins."
  - The distribution may take place in different forms, for example in a full circle at or around the altar, or lining up to receive the gifts. The distributors say the offertory words to each communicant:
    "The Body of Christ, given for you."   Amen
    "The Blood of Christ, shed for you."   Amen.
    Or: The bread of life.   Amen.
    The cup of salvation.   Amen.
- Prayer of thanksgiving

Dismissal and blessings

- Hymn
- Notices
- Prayer for peace or blessing
- Dismissal and benediction
  The congregation is sent out into daily life in accordance with the words of Martin Luther: "May the whole of your life be a service of worship". The dismissal is spoken under the promise of God's blessing, which is proclaimed to the congregation by the liturgist, often in the words of the Priestly Blessing from the Old Testament:

  "Go out in the peace of God.
  The Lord bless you and keep you.
  The Lord make his face shine on you and be gracious to you.
  The Lord lift up his countenance on you and give you peace."
  The congregation responds with "Amen", spoken once or three times.

- Postlude

7.6 Evangelical Lutheran Church in Baden (João Carlos Schmidt)

Service with communion in the Evangelical Lutheran Church in Baden – Karlsruhe Church – on 4 September 2022

1 Introduction

The Evangelical Lutheran Church in Karlsruhe holds its service with Holy Communion believing that the crucified and risen Jesus Christ – as he himself promised – is present through his word and in a special form in bread and wine at the celebration of Holy Communion. In accordance with the Lutheran Confessions, it confesses the real presence of the body and blood of Christ in the gifts of Holy Communion. With regard to brothers and sisters of other denominations, the Evangelical Lutheran Church in Baden practices eucharistic hospitality and in this sense cordially invites them to join in the celebration.

2 Order

The service with the celebration of Holy Communion in the Evangelical Lutheran congregation in Karlsruhe is based on the service order of the United Evangelical Church (VELK) and the lectionary of the Evangelical Church. 4 September is the 12th Sunday after Trinity in the Protestant church calendar.

"Joy at the presence of the crucified and risen Lord characterises Lutheran church worship. The congregation comes closer to him in the prayer of preparation at the beginning of a service, listens to his word in various readings, and responds to him in hymns and prayers, before the worshippers receive him themselves, in his body and blood, under the form of bread and wine, in Holy Communion. With the promise of his blessing, they go out again to carry it into everyday life."[99]

I. Opening and invocation

Organ prelude

Welcome with introductory thoughts on the Sunday theme

Hymn

Prayer of preparation (general confession of sins with pronouncement of absolution)

Introit (entrance psalm): from Psalm 147

Kyrie eleison

Gloria in sung form

> All glory be to God on high,
> Who hath our race befriended!
> To us no harm shall now come nigh,
> The strife at last is ended.
> God showeth His good will to men,
> And peace shall reign on earth again;
> O thank Him for His goodness!
> *(English translation: Catherine Winkworth)*

Collect of the day

---

[99] From: https://elkib.de/index.php/ueber-uns/4-gottesdienst

II. Proclamation and confession

Reading of the epistle with Hallelujah response: Acts 9: 1-20

Hymn

Gospel reading: Mark 7: 31-37

Apostolic Creed

Hymn

Sermon

Hymn

Announcements

Intercessory prayer

III. Celebration of the Holy Communion

Hymn

Preface (The Great Thanksgiving)

Sanctus

Eucharistic Prayer with Epiclesis:

We praise you, Lord of heaven and earth. You have had compassion on your creatures and sent your son as a man. We thank you for the redemption he has brought us on the cross. We beseech you: send upon us the Holy Spirit, that in this bread and wine we may receive the body and blood of Jesus Christ for our salvation, if we keep his commandments.

Words of institution

Acclamation

> Mystery of faith.
> We proclaim your death, O Lord, and profess your resurrection until you come again in glory.

Eucharistic Prayer

> So, heavenly Father, we remember your son and commemorate his suffering and death. We praise his resurrection and ascension and trust in his reign over all the earth. We beseech you: as all who receive his body are one body in Christ, so gather your Church together from the ends of the earth to celebrate with all believers the eternal feast of fellowship in

his kingdom. Through him, almighty God, in the Holy Spirit, we worship and praise, glory and honour you, now and forever, world without end. Amen.

Lord's Prayer

Agnus Dei

The Sign of Peace

Distribution with the words:

The body of Christ, given for you. / The blood of Christ, shed for you.

Nunc Dimittis (Canticle of Simeon)

Prayer of thanksgiving

IV. Dismissal and blessing

Dismissal

Blessing (Priestly Blessing)

Hymn

Organ postlude

7.7 United Methodist Church (Annette Gruschwitz and Thomas Roscher)

The Lord's Supper in the United Methodist Church (EmK) on Sunday 4 September 2022

1 Short introduction to the Methodist Worship Service[100]

Since 2017, the celebration of Holy Communion in the services of the United Methodist Church (EmK) in Germany has gained in importance. Inspired by a worship reform that has adopted numerous insights from current liturgical research and the church's own tradition, the local congregations are trying to redesign their worship around the table and to celebrate the Holy Communion as frequently as possible, both in its origin

---

[100] See "Erläuterungen zur Grundform des Gottesdienstes" on: https://emk-gottesdienst.org/besondere-zeiten/gottesdienste/gottesdienst-grundform/.

as well as repeatedly as the Lord's Supper. Thus the celebration of the Holy Communion is to be found liturgically in the third part of the service with the motto "Sharing – God connects us with one another". The basic structure of the Lord's Supper consists of the prayer before the meal (eucharistic prayer), the meal itself and the praying after the meal (thanksgiving). What is most striking about the liturgical form of the Eucharistic Prayer is the incorporation of the words of institution (*Verba Testamenti*) into the prayer of anamnetic thanksgiving. The background to this is the insight that the words of institution have been accrued into the Eucharistic Prayer as a kind of fixed narrative with an anamnetic function. If the words of institution are emphasised by special gestures or other forms, the unity of the prayer is obscured rather than promoted.[101] The dramaturgical climax of the Eucharistic Prayer is the call for the work of the Holy Spirit. In this way, the institution of the Holy Communion by Christ is liturgically reproduced by doing what he commands: eating the bread and drinking from the cup as a community gathered around the table. By doing this, the gifts are considered "consecrated", "set apart for a holy purpose..." "although they have not undergone any physical transformation."[102] The meal ends with a prayer of thanksgiving.[103]

God's word is given its audible liturgical place in the second part of the Methodist service "Listening – God speaks to us". Here, the relationship between the Bible text as it is read and as it is interpreted is redefined in diverse forms of proclamation, and is also dramaturgically staged. The worldwide Methodist Church is guided by the ecumenical pattern of three scriptural readings, taken from the Old Testament, the Epistles and the Gospels. These can be augmented by psalms at the beginning of the service or sung as hymns between the readings. However, there is no necessity to make use of a lectionary, although it is still common. In Germany, the readings and sermon texts recommended by the United Evangelical Lutheran Church (VELKD) are often chosen, because corresponding homiletic liter-

---

[101] Nevertheless, prayer gestures are not dispensed with. "The ancient biblical use of hands and arms in prayer and thanksgiving to God (...) and other gestures are ... recommended..." Das Heilige Geheimnis, Stuttgart 2005, 37f. However, it means that the *Verba Testamenti* are not specially emphasised with gestures.

[102] Ibid, 51.

[103] See on this "Erläuterungen zur Mahlfeier im Gottesdienst" at: https://emk-gottesdienst.org/besondere-zeiten/abendmahl/.

ature is to be found in German. Our worldwide Methodist Church uses the "Revised Common Lectionary" (RCL), as do many Protestant churches in North America and Canada. The RCL, like the Catholic lectionary, comprises a three-year cycle of readings, denoted A, B, and C. A text from the Gospels is read every Sunday. In year A, it is taken from the Gospel of Matthew, in year B from the Gospel of Mark, and in year C from the Gospel of Luke. The Gospel of John is read on important feast days.

Overall, the use of liturgical orders also depends on their quality and their significance for the people and the situation for which they were created. This pragmatic attitude has been inherent in the EmK from the outset. Nonetheless, it is true: "Although the freedom and diversity of Methodist worship are greater than can be represented in a single order of worship, Methodists are also attached hold to a heritage of orders and to the importance of an order of worship as a guide and template."[104] Accordingly, it is the task of competent church bodies to explore biblical and liturgical sources, and to develop liturgical forms that are appropriate for Methodists and the ecumenical perspective.[105] These forms vary because of the special character of certain feast days such as Christmas, Easter and Pentecost or other special occasions.

At the Lord's Supper, the invitation and form reflect the theological attitude of an "open Holy Communion": All who wish to encounter Jesus Christ are welcome at the Lord's Table. Christ himself, not the local congregation, is the host at the meal. Those who are aware of their own need and long for fellowship with Jesus Christ are worthy to receive communion and welcome at the Lord's Table. On the one hand, this means that baptism is not a prerequisite for participation in the celebration of the meal, but this celebration forms the basis for a conversation about baptism.[106]

---

[104] Das Heilige Geheimnis. Zum Verständnis des Abendmahls in der United Methodist Church, (EmK Forum 31) Stuttgart 2005, 40.

[105] "As stewards of the gifts given by God to the church, pastors are responsible for ensuring that the specifications for the service of the Holy Communion are observed and that the liturgical texts are used... They are found in ... liturgical material approved by the General Conference in accordance with the 'Book of Discipline', Art. 537.17 (Church Order of the worldwide Methodist Church). These liturgies are rooted in biblical, historical and ecumenical sources, and are expressions of Christian faith and worship of God." Ibid, 39.

[106] The fact that baptism as a sacrament and rite of initiation into the Christian community has been particularly strengthened and emphasised in the worldwide United

On the other hand, it means that the churches not only use wine, but also unfermented wine, grape juice or gluten-free bread or wafers, so that participation is possible for children, young people, families, sick people, and so on. Where necessary, services with a special communion liturgy are held for children, families and youth groups. In all communion services, care is taken to treat the gifts with dignity. During the whole service, the singing and music comes from Methodist and ecumenical sources from all over the world. In many cases the songs are set in several voices to make the fullness of God's praise heard.

Awareness for ecumenical and social issues is raised in the preaching, in prayer and music and also in the creeds. Apart from the Apostolic and Nicene Creeds, the Methodist Social Creed[107] is of particular importance because it emphasises the responsibility of Christians for social welfare and their commitment to loving action.

2 Liturgical ministries in worship services

One root of Methodist worship is founded in the idea of humanity as the image of God (*imago dei*). As an image, humans participate in God's glory and celebrate their creatureliness as the image of God.[108] Based on this foundation, three dimensions are ritualised in worship. These are, firstly, a "meaningful communication with God"[109], secondly a responsible treatment of creation, which includes human beings, and third, "a social existence that reflects and shares the life of the triune God."[110] Accordingly, in Methodist worship, Christians and seekers gather as a congregation to celebrate within these three dimensions and with differing responsibilities. This can be clearly seen in the different liturgical ministries, which demonstrate how the EmK implements the common priesthood and strives for the greatest possible participation of all in the service. For it is Holy Com-

---

Methodist Church in recent years is shown in: Durch Wasser und Geist. Die Taufstudie der Generalkonferenz der Evangelisch-methodistischen Kirche und die Beiträge des Nürnberger Symposiums zum Thema Taufe und Kirchengliedschaft, (EmK Forum 26) Stuttgart 2004.

[107] https://www.emk.de/glaube/typisch-methodistisch/sozial-und-politisch.
[108] Wainwright, Doxology, London 1980, 15ff.
[109] Wainright, Grundlegung des Gottesdienstes, in: Handbuch der Liturgik, Göttingen 2003, 78.
[110] Ibid.

munion and the Word of God that strengthen people for social work and mission in society.

Pastors are ordained by a bishop and are called by the church to lifelong ministry of leadership. They are commissioned to administer the sacraments (baptism and Holy Communion) according to the tradition of the church, to proclaim the gospel and to live a life of discipleship accordingly.

In addition, women and men proclaim the Word of God as lectors and lay preachers. They are given theological courses for lay people and receive ongoing training. The preaching of the gospel by lay people has made and continues to make a significant contribution to the mission of the Methodist Church.

Depending on the situation, other worshippers and church musicians contribute to the liturgy of the services. Church music is usually in the hands of volunteers.

3 Example: Order of service with Holy Communion on 4 September

ARRIVAL – God brings us together

Prelude

(The congregation stands.)

Liturgical greeting

Words of welcome

Psalm or hymn

Confession:

The liturgist says:	With thankful hearts we seek communion with God today: In his presence, we recognise and confess to God and to each other: unimportant things commanded our attention, while we took little time for the what is decisive. We were lacking in love in our actions, in our words, in our thoughts.
Congregation says:	Lord, have mercy on us. Forgive us our sins and lead us to eternal life. Amen.

Entrance prayer

(The congregation sits down.)

Hymn

LISTENING – God speaks to us

The "LISTENING" part usually contains two lessons:

Before the first lesson the lector says: The reading is taken from...

READING

After the lesson the lector says:	Word of the Living God
Congregation responds:	**Thanks be to God.**
Congregation sings:	Rejoice in the Lord... Hallelujah
Before the second lesson the lector says:	The reading is taken from the Gospel according to...

(The congregation stands.)

READING

After the lesson the lector says:	Gospel of our Lord Jesus Christ
Congregation responds:	**Praise be to you, Christ.**
Congregation sings:	Hallelujah

(The congregation sits down.)

Sermon

Time of silence

Resonance

SHARING – God connects us with one another

(The congregation stands.)

Intercessions – Lord's Prayer

(The congregation sits down.)

Hymn before the offertory

Preface

Pastor calls:	Open your hearts!
Congregation responds:	**Our hearts are open to God.**
Pastor calls:	Let us give thanks to God!
Congregation responds:	**We will gladly do so.**

(The congregation stands.)

Anamnesis

Pastor God of peace and justice,
God of freedom and mercy!
You have thoughts of peace towards us.
Suffering and pain, war and violence should not be.
You give future and hope.
Wolf and lamb shall graze together in peace.
The lion shall eat straw like the ox.
No more shall an infant live but a few days.
No evil, no crime will be done.
No one will need weapons.
The peacemakers are your children.
You comfort those who suffer.
You protect those who suffer persecution.
You can be seen by those who are pure in heart.
The merciful receive your mercy.
All of them rejoice in you.
We rejoice with them and sing:

Sanctus

Congregation sings: Holy, holy, holy

Institutio

Pastor   Through Jesus you invite us to your table.
It has been prepared in the face of our enemies.
At this table Jesus takes the bread. He praises God.
He gives thanks, breaks the bread and passes it around.
He says: Take, eat, this is my body.
Then he takes the cup.
He gives thanks, passes it around, and everyone drinks from it.
He says: Take, drink, this is my blood,
the covenant between God and his people.
And all are filled.

Epiclesis

And now: Send your Holy Spirit!
He will transform us,
as he transforms these gifts:
The bread becomes the bread of life.
The cup becomes the cup of blessing.
We become the communion of the redeemed.
Spirit of God, unite us with Christ,
unite us with one another,
unite us with creation!
Let us serve the world,
until Christ appears again.
Then he will invites us to the banquet
in God's new world.

Doxology

God of peace and justice,
God of freedom and mercy,
we give you praise and thanks for all your works.
We find shelter in your peace.
We take courage in your justice.
We are comforted by your mercy.
You gave your life for us.
Praise and thanks be to you for ever and ever!

Acclamation

With other Christians we believe:

Congregation sings:
Christ has died, / Christ is risen, / Christ will come again. Amen.

(The congregation sits down.)

Distribution

Prayer of thanksgiving

Pastor prays: Merciful God, we have tasted and seen in your meal how much you love us. For this we give you thanks.
Make us ready to live from reconciliation with you and in peace with one another.
We want to serve you with all our strength.
Preserve our joy in you despite the strain of our daily lives.
We entrust ourselves to your guidance; with you, we want to make our way confidently and joyfully.
Lead us to our end and let us be guests at the table in your kingdom.

Congregation says: Amen.

MOVING ON – God sends us out

Hymn

(The congregation stands.)

Blessing

(The congregation sits down.)

Postlude

7.8 Orthodox Churches (Marina Kiroudi)

1 Introduction to the Divine Liturgy

In the Orthodox Church, the Eucharist is at the very heart of its life and forms the central foundation of its existence. In the Eucharist, the faithful are united as members of the mystical body of Christ. This bond is not limited to the believers who participate in the Eucharist in a specific place and time. It has an eschatological dimension and extends to all members of the body of Christ without limitation of time and space. The connection even includes the Early Church and the communion with the apostles. Christ's commission at the Last Supper to share in his body and blood (Mt 26:26-28; Mk 14:22-24; Lk 22:19-20) is presently valid, just as he is still active today. In every liturgy, Christ is both the giver and the gifts.

Of all the eucharistic orders of the ancient Church, which are fundamentally known as "liturgy", the Divine Liturgy of Basil the Great and of John Chrysostom have been preserved in the Orthodox Church until today.[111] The form and wording of the liturgies go back to the Church of the first centuries and its theology, so that the liturgy is essentially a "liturgical creed"[112]. This is one decisive reason why the liturgical order is fixed and applies worldwide in the same form. It expresses the proximity to the foundation of the Christian faith and to the one undivided Church.

The celebration of the Divine Liturgy, after the preparation of the celebrants and the gifts (Proskomedia), consists of two main parts, namely the Liturgy of the Catechumens and the Liturgy of the Faithful. The Liturgy of the Catechumens is focused on the proclamation of the Word. There is a fixed order of readings which is repeated every year, starting from Easter. The sermon can be preached both by clergy as by lay people. It refers to the readings as well as to the feast day itself and can deal with current topics. The Liturgy of the Faithful is the beginning of the eucharistic liturgy, in which the gifts are changed and received. The Creed is spoken jointly before the reception of Holy Communion, which is only allowed for those

---

[111] As a rule, the liturgy of St. John Chrysostom is celebrated, while ten fixed days of the year are set aside for the liturgy of St. Basil. An exception is made for the weekdays of Great Lent before Easter. On these, the Liturgy of the Pre-Consecrated Gifts is celebrated, in which already consecrated gifts are used.

[112] Athanasios Basdekis, Die Orthodoxe Kirche. Eine Handreichung für nicht-orthodoxe und orthodoxe Christen und Kirchen, Frankfurt am Main 2007, p. 56.

who are in full church communion with the eucharistic assembly, i.e. for members of the Orthodox Church. For participation in Holy Communion it is also necessary to undergo preparation, which may take the form of prayer, fasting, penance and confession. Since individuals differ in their spiritual and physical condition, the advice and blessing of their confessor guides them in the preparation and frequency of receiving Holy Communion.

According to the order of the Early Church, the catechumens and penitents, i.e. all those who could not participate in the Eucharist, left the nave. Both in later history and in present day practice, this order is mostly not observed stringently. Particularly in places and regions with a multi-denominational population, ecumenical guests can participate in the entire liturgy – with the exception of Holy Communion. Where possible, a German translation of the service is provided for the liturgy, which is often in one or several foreign languages. At the end, as a rule, all participants in the service, whether Orthodox or non-Orthodox, are given the antidoron. This is bread which has been blessed, but not consecrated, and is distributed "instead of the actual gift" (ἀντί – in place of, δῶρον – gift), meaning the Eucharist, as a sign of union in Christ. Full church communion and unity in faith remains not only a prerequisite for eucharistic fellowship, but at the same time the ideal-typical goal of ecumenical dialogue. We remain invited to work together on this and to develop sensitivity and appreciation for one another in the process.

2 Ministries at the celebration of the Divine Liturgy

The Divine Liturgy is not only etymologically derived from the Greek term λειτουργία (λαός – people, ἔργον – work), but is also to be understood theologically as the service of the people of God. That is why the celebration of the Divine Liturgy is usually not possible without the participation of lay people. The bishop, or the priest who celebrates on behalf of the bishop, presides over the assembled congregation and offers the sacrifice at the altar. Deacons are also ordained and serve at the altar together with the bishops and priests without presiding at the eucharistic liturgy. Altar servers assist the celebrating clergy. Cantors either sing alone, intone the singing or lead a choir. Lectors read written texts aloud, such as the epistle. In practice, the roles of cantor, lector and choir are often not strictly defined.

Much of what is necessary for the liturgy takes place in the background and is hardly noticeable during the service. The prosphora, i.e. the loaves offered at the Eucharist, are either baked by parishioners who volunteer to do so or by a person appointed by the priest, depending on local tradition. Prosphora and wine are donated by the faithful. Church assistants make sure that the church is clean and orderly, and may act as contact persons for the faithful concerning practical questions during the services.

The "ordinary" people attending the service, for whom prayers are also offered during the liturgy, should not be underestimated. The "silent" participation of the believers at the liturgy is not to be equated with a passive presence, just as actionism does not necessarily mean that one is actively participating. Apart from the praise that is expressed in word, song and liturgical action, the prayer and praise of the pure heart and spirit is elemental to the service of God's people.

The Order of the Divine Liturgy of St John Chrysostom on 4 September 2022

The order of the Divine Liturgy, the readings and festive songs for this liturgical day are appointed as follows.

1. Preparation
   - Preparatory prayers of the celebrants in front of the iconostasis
   - Vesting with the liturgical garments
   - Preparation of the offertory on the preparation table in the sanctuary (Proskomedia)

2. The Litany of the Catechumens
   - Opening
     The public part of the liturgy begins with the priest's benediction: "Blessed be the kingdom of the Father and of the Son and of the Holy Spirit, now and evermore and unto the ages of ages. Amen."
   - Great Litany (Ektenia of Peace)
     The liturgy and each ektenia – as a series of intercessions is called – begins with the prayer for peace.
   - First antiphon (= call to prayer with psalm verses, repeated several times)
   - Little Litany

- Second antiphon and hymn "Only-Begotten Son
  "Only-Begotten Son and Immortal Word of God, who for our salvation didst will to be incarnate of the holy Theotokos and Ever-Virgin Mary; who without change didst become man and was crucified; who art one of the Holy Trinity, glorified with the Father and the Holy Spirit: O Christ our God, trampling down death by death, save us!"
- Little Litany
- Third Antiphon (during the Little Entrance)
  The resurrection hymn of the church tone applicable on that day is sung. The priest enters the church with the Gospel book. The entrance symbolises the beginning of Christ's public ministry.
- Hymns for the liturgical feast day (Troparion and Kontakion)
  The following hymns are appointed for this day:
  Resurrection hymn in Tone 3
  "Let the heavens rejoice! Let the earth be glad! For the Lord has shown strength with His arm! He has trampled down death by death! He has become the first-born of the dead! He has delivered us from the depths of hell, and has granted the world great mercy!"
  Festive Hymn I for the Saint's Day (Martyr Babylas, Bishop of Antioch)
  "By sharing in the ways of the Apostles, you became a successor to their throne. Through the practice of virtue, you found the way to divine contemplation, O inspired one of God; by teaching the word of truth without error, You defended the Faith, even to the shedding of your blood. Hieromartyr Babylas, entreat Christ God to save our souls."
  Festive hymn II for the Saint's Day (Prophet Moses)
  "As we celebrate the memory of Moses, your prophet, we beseech you through him, O Lord: save our souls."
  Festive hymn of the church patron (varies according to church)
  Festive hymn (Kontakion for the upcoming feast of the Nativity of Mary)
  "By your nativity, O Most Pure Virgin, Joachim and Anna are freed from barrenness; Adam and Eve, from the corruption of death. And we, your people, freed from the guilt of sin, celebrate and sing to

you: 'The barren woman gives birth to the Theotokos, the nourisher of our life!'"
- Holy God, Holy Mighty, Holy Immortal, have mercy on us. (Trisagion)
- Psalm verses before the reading (Prokimenon)
  "Sing praises to God, sing praises! Clap your hands, all peoples!" (from Ps 47)
- Epistle reading 1 Cor 15:1-11
- Alleluia with psalm verses
  "In you, O Lord, I take refuge; let me never be put to shame. Be to me a rock of refuge, my God." (from Ps 71)
- Reading from the Gospel
  Mt 16:19-26
- Sermon
- The Insistent Ektenia
- Ektenia for the catechumens and their dismissal
  At this point, prayers are spoken especially for the catechumens. At the same time, according to early Christian tradition, they are dismissed from the liturgy, even though today's practice is usually different: "All the catechumens, depart. Let none of the catechumens remain. All you faithful, let us pray to the Lord unceasingly in peace."

3. The Liturgy of the Faithful
   - Ektenia and prayers for the faithful
   - Cherubic Hymn and Great Entrance with the gifts of bread and wine
     In the Great Entrance, the priest brings the gifts to the altar. Symbolically, the incarnate Son of God himself goes to the altar as the offerer and the one who is offerered. During the Great Entrance the Cherubic Hymn is sung: "We, who mystically represent the Cherubim, And chant the thrice-holy hymn to the life-giving Trinity, let us set aside the cares of life that we may receive the King of all, who comes invisibly escorted by the Divine Hosts. Alleluia, alleluia, alleluia."
   - Litany of Supplication
   - Kiss of Peace of the celebrants and Creed

Only the Nicene-Constantinopolitan Creed (without filioque) is prayed, as was decided by the ecumenical councils and practised in the undivided Church.
- Eucharistic Anaphora
First the celebrant invites everyone: "Let us lift up our hearts". This is followed by the Thrice-Holy hymn recalling the vision of Isaiah (Is 6:1-5), since what follows forms the mystical encounter with the Lord. After this comes the institution narrative and the epiclesis, i.e. the invocation of the Holy Spirit to sanctify the gifts. After the transformation of the gifts comes the remembrance of the Mother of God and the saints, whether deceased or living, especially the local bishop, who are united in Christ.
- Supplication
- Lord's Prayer
- Greeting of Peace and prayer of prostration
The peace is offered by the priest to the congregation; the members of the congregation used to offer a formal greeting to one another before the Creed, but this is hardly ever done today.
- Elevation of the Eucharistic Bread
The Eucharistic bread is lifted up with the words, "Holiness for the holy," while the people respond, "One is holy, One is Lord, Jesus Christ, to the glory of God the Father, Amen."
- Breaking of the Eucharistic bread and mixing the wine with zeon (hot water)
The Zeon symbolises the Holy Spirit and its invigorating power.
- Communion of the celebrants (in the sanctuary)
- Communion of the faithful (in front of the iconostasis)
- The remaining eucharistic gifts are brought to the altar and then to the preparation table.
- Litany of thanksgiving after communion
- Closing prayer
- Blessing and dismissal
- Distribution of the blessed bread (antidoron)

7.9 Roman Catholic Church (Christoph Stender)

Introduction to the Eucharist

In Roman Catholic parishes, as well as in Roman Catholic organisations and institutions, the celebration of the Eucharist is vitally important.

The Second Vatican Council (1962-1965) describes the eucharistic gathering of Christians as the "the fount and apex of the whole Christian life" (Dogmatic Constitution No. 11).

The faithful are required to celebrate the Eucharist in their parish on the first day of the week, Sunday. In addition, they are invited to hear God's word every day and to celebrate the meal in remembrance of Jesus Christ.

When celebrating the Eucharist, the faithful hear the Word of God, taken from the scriptures of the Old and New Testaments. The selection of these biblical texts is based on the lectionary of the Roman Catholic Church, which is mandatory all over the world and divided into the three annual cycles of readings: A, B and C. Thus God's saving action towards his people is presented on the "Table of the Word".

Following this, the gifts of bread and wine for the meal are prepared on the altar, and the congregation gathers around it guests of Jesus Christ himself. "Christ took bread, blessed and broke it, and gave it to his disciples, saying: Take this, all of you, and eat of it, for this is my body. Do this in memory of me."[113]

The celebration of the Eucharist is characterised by a fixed procedure, which is regulated by the Missal of the Roman Catholic Church (1974) and takes into account special feast days such as Christmas, Easter and Pentecost, particular occasions such as baptism and marriage, as well as special concerns such as bereavement, thanksgiving or saints' days.

There are special forms of eucharistic celebration for target groups such as children, young people, families, the sick or the elderly. According to their specific life situations, these forms of worship include particular expressions or gestures which are appropriate, for example, for children's church or family and youth services.

---

[113] Die Feier der Heiligen Messe, Messbuch. Für die Bistümer des deutschen Sprachgebietes, p. 36 (Allgemeine Einführung).

These services create a special atmosphere through common prayer, actions and gestures of unity such as the Kiss of Peace, congregational singing or also choir or orchestra music.

As regards the sisters and brothers of other denominations who feel themselves called by Jesus Christ himself to the Holy Communion and Holy Sacrifice, the Roman Catholic liturgy aims to show ecumenical sensitivity.

In practice this means:
- Only the baptised can take part in the Eucharist and Holy Communion
- The use of the term sacrifice in liturgical language has to be examined.
- The gifts must be handled worthily.
- Hymns that are sung must be ecumenical.
- The service is to be led by a person authorised to do so.
- All the baptised should participate broadly in the liturgy.
- The "lay chalice" should be considered.

Ecumenical sensitivity is also expressed when the theme and language of the sermon correspond to this, and when the introduction to the Lord's Prayer is oriented towards multilateral ecumenism.

The celebration of the Eucharist in the Roman Catholic Church is a source of strength which helps Christians to lead their everyday lives, engage in church and social activities and seek to support the poor, oppressed and persecuted especially.

Ministries at the Eucharist

When the Eucharist is celebrated, Christians gather as a serving community united in the Holy Spirit to give thanks and praise to God.

In the local churches, special ministries are foreseen:

Lectors

The proclamation ministry lies in the hands of women and men who read the lessons from the Old and New Testament, as well as the priest who proclaims the Gospel, God's Word in human language. The congregation responds to the proclamation with an acclamation of thanks.

Intercessors

Women and men from the congregation are appointed to pray the individual intercessions, which bring before God matters of current concern within the family of humans, coupled with the request for his loving strength. Each intercession is followed by the joint petition that the prayer may be heard, often expressed with the words: "Lord in your mercy, hear our prayer".

Cantors

Their task is to lead and support the singing of the congregation at the Eucharist, or to sing the responsorial psalms with them, for example.

Altar servers

Those who have taken on altar service. Altar boys or girls (sometimes also known as acolytes) prepare the altar on behalf of the congregation together with the priest and possibly also a deacon.

Musicians

Organists accompany the singing of the congregation, but other musicians can also help to make the service dignified and festive.

Priest

The priest, ordained by the bishop and supported by the congregation, carries out the ministry of leading the celebration of the Eucharist, as a successor to the disciples called by Jesus himself.

Order of service for the eucharistic celebration

The celebration of the Eucharist on Sunday, 4 September 2022, is based on the Roman Catholic lectionary[114] for the 23rd Sunday in the Church Year with readings for the annual cycle C.

---

[114] Lectionary: The Roman Catholic lectionary prescribes which readings and which Gospel are proclaimed on a given Sunday. It unfolds the richness of Scripture in a three-year cycle of readings (A/B/C), presenting the unity of the two Testaments and the history of salvation. In this way, "the table of the Word of God" is prepared for the faithful in the Sunday services.
Church Year: The church year begins with the 1st Sunday of Advent and ends with the feast of Christ the King. It denotes a fixed sequence of feast days and festive seasons.

The following text elements are appointed for the eucharistic order of service: Collect of the day, offertory prayer and closing prayer, the readings as well as the Gospel and the Eucharistic Prayer.

Optional elements are: Opening, general confession of sin, sermon, intercessions, meditative texts, e.g. after receiving communion, and the music.

Opening

– Opening / Greeting:
The parish leader (priest) or another minister opens the service with the words: "In the name of the Father, and of the Son, and of the Holy Spirit".
– General Act of Penitence:
Joint confession of personal guilt in the face of God.
– Kyrie:
Asking for God's loving mercy.
– Gloria:
Hymn in praise of God.
– Collect of the day:
"Merciful God,
you have redeemed us through your Son
and accepted us as your beloved children.
Look with kindness on all who believe in Christ,
and give them true freedom
and the eternal inheritance.
This we ask through Jesus Christ."[115]

Celebration of the Word

– 1st reading:
Old Testament, Wis 9:13-18 (prescribed by the lectionary)
– Responsorial Psalm:
Ps 89: 3-6, 12-14 and 17 encourages the contemplation of the Word of God.

The focus is on the Church's understanding of salvation, which is expressed in the annually recurring church festivals with their services.

[115] Prescribed text from the missal. The congregation confirms this prayer, as well as the following offertory prayer and thanksgiving prayer, by the acclamation "Amen".

- 2nd reading:
  New Testament, Phlm 9b-10,12-17 (prescribed by the lectionary)
- Hallelujah:
  The assembly of believers receives and welcomes the Lord who will speak to them in the Gospel.
- Gospel:
  Lk 14: 25-33 (prescribed by the lectionary)
- Sermon:
  The sermon interprets the scripture readings according to the particular needs of the listeners from certain points of view.
- Creed:
  Common profession of the Christian faith
- Intercessions:
  Supplicatory prayer for the concerns of humanity, of the churches and for personal cares.

Meal celebration

- Offertory preparation:
  The altar is prepared with the gifts of bread and wine.
- Offertory Prayer:
  "Lord our God,
  you give us peace
  and give us the strength to serve you sincerely.
  Let us honour you with our gifts
  and be of one mind through the participation
  on the one bread and the one cup.
  This we ask through Christ our Lord."[116]
- Eucharistic Prayer:
  The Eucharistic Prayer with the words of institution (consecration) – this prayer of thanksgiving and sanctification is the centre and climax of the whole celebration. This also includes the Sanctus, with which the entire congregation is united with the heavenly hosts. (The wording is prescribed in the missal.)
- Lord's Prayer:

---

[116] Prescribed text from the missal.

In the Lord's Prayer we ask for our daily bread, which reminds Christians above all of the Eucharistic bread, and for deliverance from sins, so that holiness may truly be given to the holy.
- Sign of Peace:
In words and gestures, the congregation asks God for peace and unity,
- Breaking of bread:
The breaking of the Eucharistic bread is accompanied by the response of the congregation, "Lamb of God..." (Agnus Dei).
- Communion:
The congregation is invited to receive Jesus Christ in the form of bread, which is offered with the words "the body of Christ" or "the bread of life". The communicant "confirms" this with the acclamation Amen. There is also the possibility of chalice communion ("lay chalice").
- Prayer of thanksgiving:
"Lord our God,
in your word and sacrament
you have given us food and life.
Let us grow in love
through these great gifts
and reach eternal communion
with your son,
who lives and reigns with you for ever and ever."[117]

Conclusion

- Blessing:
The priest asks for God's blessing on the congregation "in the name of the Father, and of the Son, and of the Holy Spirit."
- Dismissal: The congregation responds to the invitation to "Go in peace" with "Thanks be to God", in order to return to everyday life with renewed strength.

---

[117] Prescribed text from the missal.

8 Diversity of liturgies – a brief overview

(Hacik Gazer, Markus Iff, Werner Klän and Dorothea Sattler)

8.1 Formation of liturgical traditions in East and West

Today, there is a wide range of different kinds of Christian worship on Sundays and feast days, as well as on many weekdays. Their current form is bases on a long history which cannot be easily reconstructed. Especially for the first decades of Christian congregations, it is not possible to gain a reliable overview of their liturgies. It can be assumed that there was a great variety of celebration forms in the early period. Later, types of worship emerged that had greater or lesser similarities. As Christianity spread further and further afield, fixed Christian forms and orders of worship gradually developed in further parts of the oikumene/world (West and East, North and South). They were celebrated in different languages, depending on the region. They also had extremely various musical forms. All Christian services, then as now, share the individual elements of the service: invocation, thanksgiving, praise, lamentation, intercession, scripture readings, sermon, blessing. All over the world, the gospel has been testified in manifold ways for generations. It is in the Christian church services that its proclamation is most intensely expressed.

Over the centuries, various liturgical centres and territories were established, first in eastern and western parts of the Roman Empire, and then further abroad. The Eastern liturgies include the forms of worship that originated in what is now Egypt, Ethiopia, Syria, Armenia, Georgia, Persia, Iraq, Palestine, Lebanon and Israel and spread out from these countries and regions. For the entire Orthodox Churches of the Byzantine-Slavic tradition, including the Eastern Catholic Churches, the Byzantine Rite of Constantinople still exists today, although it originally has its roots in Antioch in western Syria. Today, all Orthodox churches celebrate their services according to this rite.

The Western liturgies originated in the countries we know today as: Italy (Rome, Milan, Aquileia, Ravenna), Ireland, Spain, France and North Africa. They were also held in different languages, Latin, Gothic or Old Spanish. The Franco-Roman liturgy developed out of the rite of the city of Rome, the papal Masses and the Old Gallic rite, each with its own branches for individual dioceses as well as for the monastic orders.

The differences between the liturgical traditions in the East and the West, which became apparent from early times, were never a cause of controversy in themselves because of the diversity that was lived. However, differences in christological and ecclesiological doctrine influenced the celebration of services – for example, because of differences in the Creed (originally without and only in the Latin versions with filioque) or also with regard to the naming of church leaders, in communion with whom the Eucharist could be celebrated.

8.2 Service reform

A particular concern of the ecumenical movement is lasting reform. In the area of liturgies, too, the continual aim is to find a consistent connection between meaning and form of worship services. In this endeavour, confessional traditions are always learning from one another. At the same time, it must be noted that many believers in Christ hardly have an insight into the liturgies of other denominations. It is to be hoped that the mutual awareness of worship traditions will increase. The realisation of a constant reform of the services is ecumenically relevant.

8.2.1 Reforms in the realm of Protestant churches

In the area of the Wittenberg Reformation, Martin Luther developed fundamental reforms of the traditional Mass celebration, first with the Formula Missae (1523), then with the German Mass (1526). Above all, he eradicated the canon from the order of service. Variations of these forms became established in the orders of Reformation churches, especially in central and northern Germany and Denmark. In Sweden, the reform of the Mass was more conservative. In the area of the Swiss Reformation, the sermon was predominant at the services; baptism and the Holy Communion were inserted as supplementary elements here and there. John Calvin's liturgies were largely decisive here. In the Netherlands, models drafted by John Laski were further developed. In Scotland, John Knox was instrumental in laying the foundation for the later Book of Common Order. All in all, we can speak of a variety of forms of worship in the Reformation churches. In the 17th and 18th centuries there were crises in worship, and as a result numerous private orders emerged. Efforts towards standardisation, expressed for example in the Protestant unions in the 19th century, did not fundamentally interrupt this tendency towards pluralisation. In the 20th century, the liturgical movement also sought to integrate aspects of ecumenism and of church music. In the last decades of the 20th century, social changes led to new forms of worship services going beyond the traditional ones. More recent conceptions are trying to bind these different elements together into a basic structure with greater variability.

The Protestant free churches have their historical and theological roots in the Reformation. Their services are usually closer to the model of the Upper German service of the Word, rather than to the tradition of the Mass. In comparison to the German Protestant regional churches, some special characteristics of free church services are recognisable. The fellowship of the congregation gathered in the name of Jesus Christ is particularly emphasised. Regular attendance at church leads to a lively participation in the service by the congregation; apart from taking on liturgical functions, the worshippers bring personal testimonies of faith and life. For this purpose, some free church traditions have firmly established a special time of fellowship. There is a reluctance to use fixed agendas, but this does not express disdain for worship, but rather a rejection of prescribed texts, so that there is no restriction for the free working of the Spirit and the personal expression of piety. The sermon is held in high esteem in free church services and is characterised by both biblical interpretation and relevance to everyday life. Apart from the pastors, who are theologically trained and usually ordained, volunteer lay preachers regularly hold the sermons. It may not apply equally to all free churches, but music, songs of praise, and congregational singing frequently play a central role. Many free church congregations have bands that lead the congregation in songs of praise and adoration. Holy Communion (also called the Lord's Supper), is usually held once a month, either as an integral part of the service or following it. In principle, it is open to all who live in a faith relationship with Jesus Christ, even if they belong to a different church.

8.2.2 Reforms in the realm of the Roman Catholic Church

In the Roman Catholic Church today, the recognition of liturgical diversity is in principle undisputed. The 2nd Vatican Council (1962-65) supported the request to allow cultural influences and especially the use of the respective mother tongue in the worship services (cf. 2nd Vatican Council, Sacrosanctum Concilium 37-40). The Latin liturgical language, which up to the 2nd Vatican Council had been preserved since medieval times, was originally intended to express the worldwide unity of Roman Catholics; however, this liturgical tradition meant that a lively participation of the faithful in the celebration was strictly limited. For many people, the biblical texts recited in Latin were incomprehensible.

Many of the issues formulated in the Constitution on the Liturgy of Vatican II recall ideas of the 16th-century Reformation: the active participation of all people in the liturgical assembly; listening to God's Word as interpreted by people trained and commissioned to do so; the presence of Jesus Christ in the assembled congregation; the mutual connection between the liturgy of the Word and the celebration of Mass.

The Roman Catholic tradition also expresses its esteem for the proclamation of the biblical Word of God in the celebration of the Eucharist by prescribing an order of readings (lectionary) that is valid in the entire worldwide Church. The challenge of not being able to make one's own choice of a scriptural text to preach on, but rather to be given a guideline that forces the preacher to be first of all a listener, seems important here. In addition, the globally binding reading order forms a fellowship: people in all places are listening to the same Word of God.

9 Suggestions for an ecumenically sensitive liturgical practice

9.1 Basic thoughts

There is evidence that many Christians are not familiar with the liturgical practice of other churches. Meeting each other is the prerequisite for forming an ecumenical commitment. Visiting other denominations' places of worship, standing beside the baptismal font or discovering the week's service schedule in newsletters or on notice boards can strengthen ecumenical awareness. There is still much to be discovered in ecumenical solidarity: the appearance of the church interior, the vestments and other utensils used at the services, the pictures on the walls, the lectern and pulpit, or musical traditions.

It is a common ecumenical conviction that the proclamation of the Word of God is a constitutive element of the liturgy. It would be a good thing if the readings appointed in the various denominational lectionaries were basically to be used in some form in all Sunday liturgies (by being read aloud, or referred to in the sermon, or in another context during the service). In this way, one could draw attention to all that we have in common in biblical proclamation.

Discussing how important the celebration of the Holy Communion, Eucharist and Holy Sacrifice is to people personally is an enrichment for all who take part in such conversations. Holding ecumenical house groups could be one way of finding such personal spiritual enrichment.

The celebration of Holy Communion, Eucharist and Holy Sacrifice has a strong connection to diakonia, the Christian social work. In the biblical tradition, this is expressed in the story of Jesus' feet washing, and in the warning not to let the Lord's Supper lead to social tension. Locally, there are many possibilities to give creative and imaginative shape to the relationship between liturgy and diakonia in ecumenical solidarity.

9.2 Practical examples

It is in keeping with the aims of the ecumenical movement that all services should always be celebrated in an ecumenically sensitive way. The following, very specific suggestions may be helpful in this regard.

9.2.1 Participation of members of the congregation

Overall, attention should be paid to a strong participation of parishioners in order to make it clear that the whole congregation celebrates Holy Communion, Eucharist or Holy Sacrifice. For this reason, pastors, priests, deacons (if applicable), lectors, cantors and all those who have a special task in the liturgy should process into the church together and then, if possible, sit together near the altar. In this way the church can be visibly seen to be gathered around the altar or altar table, symbolising the presence of Christ. The person who is officially appointed or authorised to lead the celebration is then recognisably part of the congregation. The liturgy should make clear that the baptised and believing Christians gathered there are celebrating the Holy Communion and Eucharist together.

9.2.2 Selection of songs

In all regional liturgies there is great freedom in the choice of hymns. There are obviously always opportunities to include ecumenical hymns, and singing songs in other languages can draw attention to the worldwide extent of the Christian church.

9.2.3 Liturgy of the Word

Christianity is united by the Holy Scriptures of the Old and New Testaments. The Bible is the common document of faith. This could be expressed, for example, by inviting Christians of other denominations to act as lectors in the readings from the Old and New Testaments.

The themes, theological statements, language, etc. should be chosen in such a way that they are enriching for the faithful of other denominations and helpful for ecumenical togetherness.

9.2.4 Creed, Lord's Prayer and Blessing

The Creed and the Lord's Prayer are the confession and the prayer that unite the Christian churches. At the same time, in every church and for every individual these texts are central and well-known from the liturgy and the Bible. They unite Christianity and mark the connection between baptism and the Eucharist. The Creed is part of the baptismal liturgy, as is the Lord's Prayer. A further part of the service is God's blessing, which believers in Christ seek and beseech, both for themselves as well as for Christianity throughout the world. A short sentence to introduce the blessing can remind us of this and place the following form of benediction in the context of ecumenism.

9.2.5 Intercessory prayer

At the intercessions it should be a matter of course to offer petitions for the other Christian churches, especially in the context of an ecumenical event. In addition, as with the readings, it is possible to ask believers from other churches to join in reading the prayers. It would be a good sign of ecumenical togetherness if neighbouring congregations or ecumenically committed groups were to join in preparing the intercessory prayer for the liturgies on Sunday.

9.2.6 Ecumenically sensitive design of the meal celebration

In order to emphasise that the liturgy of the word and the celebration of the meal are separate parts of the service, it might make sense not to set the altar or communion table until the beginning of the communion or Eucharist.

All prayers spoken at Holy Communion, Eucharist and Holy Sacrifice must be examined to see whether the reference to sacrifice corresponds to the ecumenical convergences achieved: Christ Jesus himself is the subject of the eucharistic event. All those taking part are invited and called upon to live in such a way that they offer their lives out of love for all creatures (Romans 12:1).

The invocation of the Holy Spirit to transform both the hearts of the assembled congregation and the gifts at the table, which become the sign of reconciliation in Christ, is a well-known element of many Christian liturgies and is practised by many congregations.

The eucharistic celebration with bread and wine corresponds to the institution by Jesus Christ. It has become a painful sign of division that the chalice is not given to lay people. There are no dogmatic obstacles, even in the Roman Catholic liturgy, to respecting Jesus Christ's commission: "Drink from it, all of you" – as is regular practice both in the Protestant and Orthodox liturgies

All denominations share the conviction that the original meaning of Jesus' words about bread and wine at the meal of the assembled believers is a sign of reconciliation and communion. At the same time, some traditions have preserved forms of keeping the gifts of the meal for later celebration with sick and elderly people. Mutual ecumenical respect demands meticulous handling of the gifts from the meal (for example, by consuming them after the celebration in a small group). It would be satisfying to strengthen the ecumenical practice of going together to sick and elderly people after communion and Eucharist in order to allow them to share in the fellowship.

9.2.7 Commemoration of the dead

All those who are baptised live in paschal hope. In the local context, prayerful commemoration of the deceased from other denominations is a sign of communion in faith. Such a sign could be the naming of those who have passed away in the local parishes during the period of the 3rd Ecumenical Kirchentag, accompanied by a prayer for them. In particular, the commemoration of the martyrs, saints and confessors should be considered with regard to their broad ecumenical significance.

9.2.8 Respect for the ordained ministry and special ministries

In the ecumenical movement as a whole, there seems little prospect of finding visible unity among the churches if the question of ministry is not discussed. It was possible to achieve important rapprochements in the ecumenical dialogues. The commissioning of theologically trained persons called by God for the public proclamation of the gospel and the celebration of the sacraments, who are ordained with prayer and the laying on of hands, serves the concern for the safeguarding of the one gospel of Jesus Christ proclaimed in the apostolic tradition. It would therefore be desirable that only ordained persons, or those entrusted with the administration of the sacraments or the Holy Communion in their churches, should preside over the Holy Communion and the Eucharist. In Protestant free churches, leading or presiding over the service of Holy Communion is not the exclusive prerogative of the ordained ministry, but is usually entrusted to people appointed to do so (pastors, elders, deacons). Nevertheless, they recognise that the commissioning by ordination of theologically trained persons called by God to publicly proclaim the gospel and celebrate the sacraments serves the concern for the safeguarding of the one gospel of Jesus Christ proclaimed in the apostolic tradition.

According to the Lutheran confessions, the ecclesiastical ministry is assigned to serve the means of grace, not as a third one in addition to Word and Sacrament, but existing for their sake. Since the 19th century, the distinction between "priesthood of all baptised/believers" and "ordained ministry" has also been disputed in the churches of the Lutheran Concord. However, against the background of the XIV Article of the Augsburg Confession, it is true that the leadership of the worship service, especially the administration of the sacrament, is reserved for the ordained, elected and instituted pastor.

9.2.9 Baptism and Holy Communion, Eucharist and Holy Sacrifice

In the Christian denominations, there have recently been differing theological positions on the question of whether the celebration of the Eucharist is only possible for people who have already been baptised. In ecumenism, the conviction is often shared that participating people can agree inwardly to the meaning of the liturgical celebration. People who are seeking for Jesus Christ differ in this case from adherents of other religions who, from their point of view, are for good reasons unable to share the confession of Jesus Christ. The eucharistic celebration is not to be confused with a meal of thanksgiving for the gifts of creation.

9.2.10 Eucharistic Liturgy and Agape

The distinction between the liturgical remembrance of Christ in the Holy Communion or Eucharist and the everyday table fellowship to satisfy hunger has a long tradition. The New Testament already bears witness to the problem that the combination of both forms of the meal led to social tensions, because poor people could only come later and had to eat what was left over. At the same time, the inner connection between Eucharist and Agape has always been preserved in order to give tangible substance to the spiritual connection between the remembrance of Christ and life in reconciled fellowship.

10 Authors

Bosse-Huber, Petra
Petra Bosse-Huber, born 1959, Protestant theologian, since 2014 Head of the Department "Ecumenical Relations and Ministries Abroad" in the Church Office of the Evangelical Church in Germany (EKD) in Hanover and thus Bishop for foreign relations of the EKD; Vice-President of the Church Office of the EKD; Head of the Office of the Union of Evangelical Churches in the Church Office of the EKD; Member of the Central and Executive Committee of the World Council of Churches (WCC), the Presidium of the German Protestant Kirchentag (DEKT) and the Conference on Diakonie and Development of the EKD.

Durber, Susan
Susan Durber, born in 1960, is a minister in the United Reformed Church in the United Kingdom. She has exercised her ministry in various parts of England, as Principal of Westminster College, Cambridge and as Theological Advisor for Christian Aid. Since 2014 she has been Moderator of the Faith and Order Commission of the World Council of Churches and in this context has been involved in numerous ecumenical dialogue and study processes with presentations and publications.

Easthill, Christopher
Christopher Easthill, born 1960, Anglican theologian; since 2014 parish priest at the Church of St Augustine of Canterbury in Wiesbaden; co-chair of the Council of Anglican Episcopal Churches in Germany; member of the board of the Council of Churches in Germany; member of the Dialogue Commission of the Evangelical Lutheran Church in Bavaria and The Episcopal Church.

Gazer, Hacik
Hacik Rafi Gazer, born 1963, Armenian Apostolic theologian. Since 2006 Professor of History and Theology of Eastern Christianity at the

Faculty of Philosophy and Department of Theology of the Friedrich-Alexander-University Erlangen-Nürnberg. Since 1996 Official Delegate of the Diocese of the Armenian Church in Germany to the Council of Churches in Germany ACK and since 2006 member of the German Ecumenical Studies Committee DÖSTA. Since 2015 Chairman of the Diocesan Delegate Assembly of the Diocese of the Armenian Church in Germany.

Gruschwitz, Annette
Annette Gruschwitz, born 1976, Dr, pastor and head of the Committee for Worship and Agenda of the United Methodist Church in Germany.

Iff, Markus
Markus Iff, born 1964, Protestant and Free Church theology; pastor in the Federation of Free Evangelical Churches; since 2011 Professor of Systematic Theology and Ecumenics at the Theological Seminary of Ewersbach in Dietzhölztal. Research and work focus, among other things, on denominational studies, ecclesiology, understanding of ministry in a free church and ecumenical perspective.

Kiroudi, Marina
Marina Kiroudi, Orthodox theologian; since 2022 research assistant for religious education at the University of Bonn; until 2022 Orthodox advisor to the Council of Churches in Germany.

Klän, Werner
Werner Klän, born 1952, pastor of the Independent Evangelical Lutheran Church (SELK); 1993-2002 Professor of Church History, 2002-2018 of Systematic Theology at the Lutheran Theological Seminary Oberursel, since 1993 member of the German Ecumenical Study Committee; 2012-2018 Associate Professor at the University of Pretoria; 2013-2019 Lutheran Co-Chair in the informal academic dialogue between the International Lutheran Council and the Pontifical Council for Promoting Christian Unity, Chair of the Diaspora Work in the SELK-"Gotteskasten" association. Concerned with questions of confessional, Lutheran and ecumenical theology.

Meister, Julia
Julia Meister, born 1991, Protestant theologian; 2020-2021 project coordinator at the 3rd Ecumenical Kirchentag; 2017-2020 research assistant at the Institute for Hermeneutics and Dialogue of Cultures at the

University of Tübingen; since 2022 appointed advisor in the "Theology, Pastoral and Ecumenism" department at the Central Committee of German Catholics (ZdK); PhD project: Church in Civil Society. The unconditional prerequisites of democracy and their formation in the church.

Miron, Radu Constantin

Radu Constantin Miron, born 1956, is a Greek Orthodox theologian; Byzantine, Romance and Theology studies in Thessaloniki, Bonn and Cologne; MTh University of Thessaloniki (2010); 1983 to 2016 priest of the Greek Orthodox parish in Brühl; at the same time 1998 to 2003 priest in Düsseldorf and Eupen; since 2016 parish priest in Cologne; Vicar Bishop of the Romanian parishes of the Greek Orthodox Metropolis; since 1985 Archpriest; Archpriest of the Ecumenical Patriarchate of Constantinople since 2004; worked as teacher of religious education and prison chaplain, as well as lecturer in the Master of Ecumenical Studies programme at the University of Bonn; Ecumenism Secretary of the Greek Orthodox Metropolis of Germany; Commissioner of the Orthodox Bishops' Conference for Christian relations; since 2019 chairman of the Council of Churches in Germany.

Pfützner, Joachim

Joachim Pfützner, born 1953, Dipl. theol., until his retirement in July 2019 priest of the Old Catholic parish of Stuttgart; since 2007 member of the Liturgical Commission of the Diocese of Old Catholics in Germany, since 2019 as chairman, since 2012 lecturer for liturgical studies in the Master's programme Old Catholic and Ecumenical Theology of the Old Catholic Seminary of the Rheinische Friedrich-Wilhelms-Universität Bonn.

Roscher, Thomas

Thomas Roscher, born 1961, Dr. theol., pastor and Commissioner for Worship and Agendas of the United Methodist Church in Germany.

Sattler, Dorothea

Dorothea Sattler, born 1961, Roman Catholic theologian; Professor of Ecumenical Theology and Dogmatics at the University of Münster since 2000; Scientific Director of the Ecumenical Working Group of Protestant and Catholic Theologians; Member of the German Ecumenical Study Committee; Facilitator at "Global Ecumenical Theological Institute" (GETI) WCC Karlsruhe 2022; Spokesperson for "Theology, Pastoral and Ecumenism" at the Central Committee of German Catholics (ZdK); involved in synodal reform movements of the Roman Catholic Church, especially with regard to the participation of women in ministries and offices in the Church.

Schmidt, João Carlos

João Carlos Schmidt, born 1967, comes from the Evangelical Lutheran Church of Brazil (IELB). Theological studies, ordination and first pastorate in the church there. From 1998 to 2004 he completed his doctorate in Missiology and Religious Studies at the Faculty of Theology of Erlangen University. During and after his doctorate, he held various positions in church and academic fields. Since January 2017 pastor of the Evangelical Lutheran Church in Baden in Karlsruhe. Deputy superintendent since March 2018.

Stender, Christoph

Christoph Stender, born 1957, Roman Catholic theologian, priest in the Diocese of Aachen; since 2017 Spiritual Rector in the Central Committee of German Catholics (ZdK) and managing director of "Theology, Pastoral and Ecumenism" in the ZdK; delegate of the German Bishops' Conference in the General Assembly of the Council of Churches in Germany (ACK); involved in issues of religious education and communication, as well as in the synodal path in the Roman Catholic Church.

Uphoff, Frank

Frank Uphoff, born 1960, married to Petra, four adult children. Since 2017 leading pastor of the Christus Gemeinde Velbert and since 2012 Vice-President of the Association of Pentecostal Churches in Germany (BFP). After theological studies at the Erzhausen Theological Seminary (until 1984), trainee in Griesheim near Darmstadt, later pastor there (until 1994). Pastor of the ARCHE Free Church in Augsburg (until 2005), then pastor of the Christian Free Church Munich and leader of the BFP region Bavaria-South. BFP delegate to the Council of Churches in Germany (ACK) and the Association of Evangelical Free Churches (VEF), where he is also a board member. Vice-chairman of the Evangelical Alliance in Velbert. Editor of the internet portal lehrmaterial.net with spiritual study material.

Ökumenische Studien / Ecumenical Studies
hrsg. von Prof. Dr. Ulrich Becker (Universität Hannover), Prof. Dr. Erich Geldbach (Marburg), Prof. Dr. Rebekka Klein (Universität Bochum) Prof. Dr. Ulrike Link-Wieczorek (Universität Oldenburg), Prof. Dr. Gottfried Orth (TU Braunschweig, Ernst Lange-Institut Rothenburg), Prof. Dr. Konrad Raiser (Genf/Berlin), und Prof. Dr. Dorothea Sattler (Universität Münster)

Hans-Martin Barth
Eins und Amen
Ein ökumenisch-interreligiöses Tagebuch
Ökumene lebt von Freundschaften und Begegnungen, aber auch von Beheimatung in der eigenen wie in fremden Traditionen. Noch mehr als die Ökumene braucht der interreligiöse Dialog Neugier, Offenheit, gegenseitige Einladungen und wissenschaftlichen Austausch. Erfahrungen, in vier Jahrzehnten gewonnen, präsentiert Hans-Martin Barth in Auszügen aus seinen Tagebüchern. Er grüßt damit Freunde und Gleichgesinnte und ermutigt spirituell engagierte Menschen, sich persönlich auf ökumenische und interreligiöse Prozesse einzulassen.
Bd. 51, 2022, 368 S., 34,90 €, br., ISBN 978-3-643-15063-9

Michael Plathow
Faszination Ökumene
Sternstunden, Meilensteine, Wegmarken und Kompass des ökumenischen Wegs
Bd. 50, 2022, ca. 216 S., ca. 29,90 €, br., ISBN 978-3-643-14767-7

Sentus Francis Dikwe
Remembering the Dead
The Reception of African Tradition of Ancestorship in an Ecumenical Context
Bd. 49, 2021, 320 S., 39,90 €, br., ISBN 978-3-643-91281-7

Evodius Mbenna
The Sacrament of the Eucharist in Intercultural Ecumenical Communication
Joseph Ratzinger and Walter Kasper as Inspirers for the Ecumenical Dialogue in Africa
Bd. 48, 2021, 290 S., 34,90 €, br., ISBN 978-3-643-91261-9

J. Denny Weaver
Gewaltfreie Erlösung
Kreuzestheologie im Ringen mit der Satifaktionstheorie. Übersetzt aus dem Englischen von Jürg Bräker, unter Mitarbeit der „Arbeitsstelle Theologie der Friedenskirchen" der Universität Hamburg. Geleitwort von Fernando Enns
Bd. 47, 2016, 386 S., 34,90 €, br., ISBN 978-3-643-13226-0

Ulrich Schmitthenner; Peter Schönhöffer; Christoph Grosse (Hg.)
Die Zukunft, die wir meinen – Leben statt Zerstörung
Ökumenische Versammlung Mainz 2014
Bd. 46, 2015, 230 S., 24,90 €, br., ISBN 978-3-643-12869-0

Rüdiger With
Pneuma und Amt
Ökumenische Reflexionen im Anschluss an Walter Kasper
Bd. 45, 2015, 296 S., 34,90 €, br., ISBN 978-3-643-12842-3

LIT Verlag Berlin – Münster – Wien – Zürich – London
Auslieferung Deutschland / Österreich / Schweiz: siehe Impressumsseite

Studien zur systematischen Theologie und Ethik
gegründet von Prof. Dr. E. Lessing(†), Prof. Dr. P. Neuner, Prof. Dr. Dres. h. c. D. Ritschl, D. D. (†)
hrsg. von Prof. M. Beintker (Universität Münster), Prof. R. Bernhardt (Universität Basel), Prof. R. Miggelbrink (Universität Duisburg-Essen), Prof. P. Neuner (Universität München), und Prof. B. Stubenrauch (Universität München)

Jihoon Yoon
Motive und Entwicklung der atheistischen Religionskritik
Eine apologetische Studie ausgehend von Wolfhart Pannenberg
Karl Marx (1844) betrachtete Ludwig Feuerbach als erfolgreichen Abschluss der atheistischen Religionskritik. Nicht nur mit Friedrich Nietzsche und Sigmund Freud, sondern auch mit Charles Darwin bekam sie jedoch neue Impulse, bis hin zu den „Four Horsemen" (Richard Dawkins, Daniel Clement Dennett, Sam Harris, Christopher Hitchens), die nicht nur im angelsächsischen Raum Furore machten. Jihoon Yoon analysiert diese Spur in seiner Studie und zeichnet sorgfältig Motive und Argumente des alten wie des neuen Atheismus nach. Dabei orientiert er sich an der Systematischen Theologie Wolfhart Pannenbergs, die sich offensiv verstand, aber auch als eine Form der Apologetik interpretiert und gegen den Neuen Atheismus argumentativ ausgewertet werden kann.
Bd. 71, 2021, 480 S., 59,90 €, br., ISBN 978-3-643-15056-1

André Jeromin
„Es wird regiert ... "
Gottes Weltregierung als Teil der *providentia Dei* nach Karl Barth
In biblischen Erzählungen und christlicher Tradition scheint ausgemacht, dass Gott die Welt aktiv regiert. Gleichzeitig fällt es vielen Menschen schwer, ihre Autonomieerfahrung und die Vorstellung von Gottes Eingreifen in den Weltverlauf zu vereinbaren. Wie kann diese Spannung überbrückt werden? Karl Barths „Kirchliche Dogmatik" antwortet auf diese Frage. Die vorliegende Untersuchung erschließt diese Antwort in ihren situativen Kontexten und zeigt ihr Potenzial auf, um ausgehend von Barths Entwurf Impulse zu geben, wie Gottes Regieren in unserer Zeit verstanden werden kann.
Bd. 70, 2021, 644 S., 79,90 €, br., ISBN 978-3-643-14900-8

Henry Chukwudi Okeke
The Spirituality of the Igbo People of Nigeria as an Example of Religious Modernization in a Global World
If there is no religion in the world, the world would more or less become a jungle. The world will be inhuman. Religion touches all aspects of human life. Identifying God's will in our world today has become a major problem for many religions of the world. In the past, in Igbo Traditional Religion, human sacrifice as well as the killing of twins were practised. For the Igbo traditionalists then, that was the will of the deities and equally not against God's will. But following the encounter of Igbo Traditional Religion with Christianity these are no longer practised.
Misinterpretation of God's will by some religions of the world has given rise to religious violence, religious extremism, fanaticism and terrorism we are experiencing today in the world. For these problems to be resolved, it is pertinent that the study of various religions be taken seriously. This study should be aiming at better understanding, co-existence, respect for one another and frequent interreligious dialogues among the various religions of the world. When this is achieved, the believers of various religions would realize that many are worshipping one God and their desire is to communicate with Him, although they may approach Him differently.
Bd. 69, 2019, 420 S., 39,90 €, br., ISBN 978-3-643-91109-4

Christiane Tjaden
Politik im Gebet
Erträge Dietrich Bonhoeffers und Karl Barths für eine Theologie der Fürbitte für den Staat
Bd. 68, 2017, 298 S., 34,90 €, br., ISBN 978-3-643-13708-1

Ivo Bäder-Butschle
Brüchige Fundamente
Eine Revision der Rechtfertigungslehre
Bd. 67, 2017, 238 S., 29,90 €, br., ISBN 978-3-643-13671-8

LIT Verlag Berlin – Münster – Wien – Zürich – London
Auslieferung Deutschland / Österreich / Schweiz: siehe Impressumsseite

Religion – Geschichte – Gesellschaft
Fundamentaltheologische Studien
begründet von Prof. Dr. Dr. Johann Baptist Metz (†), Prof. Dr. Jürgen Werbick,
Prof. Dr. Johann Reikerstorfer
hrsg. von Prof. Dr. Ulrich Engel OP (Institut M.-Dominique Chenu, Berlin), Prof. Dr. Judith Gruber (KU Leuven), Dr. Michael Hoelzl (University of Manchester)

Stephan Tautz
Radikale Sakramentalität
William T. Cavanaughs politische Theologie der Eucharistie im Gespräch mit radikaldemokratischer Theorie der Macht
Stephan Tautz geht in seiner Studie der Frage nach, inwieweit sich Sakramentalität als Paradigma für eine subversive Wende der politischen Theologie denken lässt. Den Ausgangspunkt bildet dabei die politische Theologie des US-amerikanischen Theologen William T. Cavanaugh, in deren Zentrum die Eucharistie als liturgische Konstitution der Kirche steht. Diesen sakramentalen Zugang erweitert der Autor konstruktiv um die radikaldemokratische Interpretation der Macht als Leerstelle und stellt damit die Frage nach einem transformierten politischen Kirchenverständnis für heute.
Bd. 56, 2022, ca. 400 S., ca. 49,90 €, br., ISBN 978-3-643-15130-8

Leonardo Boff
Gottes Leidenschaft mit den Armen – Der Gott der kleinen Leute
Zwischenbilanz 50 Jahre Theologie der Befreiung. Deutsche Übersetzung Bruno Kern.
Mit einem Vorwort von Jürgen Moltmann
Es ist ein einmaliger Vorgang innerhalb der mehr als zweitausendjährigen Geschichte der christlichen Kirchen: Zum ersten Mal entsteht ein grundlegender theologischer Neuansatz, ein neues Paradigma für das theologische Denken insgesamt, an der Peripherie der Weltgesellschaft und der Kirche. Die eigentlichen Subjekte dieser Theologie sind die Armen, ihre Gemeinden und Selbstorganisationen. Nach 50 Jahren beschreibt einer der Väter dieser neuen Theologie, Leonardo Boff, diesen radikalen Standortwechsel und zeigt anhand zweier zentraler Herausforderungen auf, wie sich die Befreiungstheologie selbst weiterentwickelt hat.
Bd. 55, 2021, 108 S., 19,90 €, br., ISBN 978-3-643-91307-4

Alexandra Lason
Umstrittenes Abendland
Eine theologische Grundlagenreflexion
Bd. 53, 2021, 386 S., 49,90 €, br., ISBN 978-3-643-14650-2

Daniel Bugiel
Diktatur des Relativismus?
Fundamentaltheologische Auseinandersetzung mit einem kulturpessimistischen Deutungsschema
Bd. 52, 2021, 304 S., 39,90 €, br., ISBN 978-3-643-14593-2

Joachim Negel
Feuerbach weiterdenken
Studien zum religionskritischen Projektionsargument
Bd. 51, 2014, 504 S., 59,90 €, br., ISBN 978-3-643-12583-5

Hans-Gerd Janßen; Julia D. E. Prinz; Michael J. Rainer (Hg..)
Theologie in gefährdeter Zeit
Stichworte von nahen und fernen Weggefährten für Johann Baptist Metz zum 90. Geburtstag
Bd. 50, 2. Aufl. 2019, 600 S., 39,90 €, br., ISBN 978-3-643-14106-4

LIT Verlag Berlin – Münster – Wien – Zürich – London
Auslieferung Deutschland / Österreich / Schweiz: siehe Impressumsseite

Vergessene Theologen

Peter Browe

Die Eucharistie im Mittelalter

Liturgiehistorische Forschungen
in kulturwissenschaftlicher Absicht

Mit einer Einführung
herausgegeben von Hubertus Lutterbach
und Thomas Flammer

7. Auflage 2019

Vergessene Theologen Bd. 1
LIT

Peter Browe
Die Eucharistie im Mittelalter
Liturgiehistorische Forschungen in kulturwissenschaftlicher Absicht. Mit einer Einführung herausgegeben von Hubertus Lutterbach und Thomas Flammer
Der Jesuit und Liturgiewissenschaftler Peter Browe (†1949) war nach seinem Tod über Jahrzehnte hinweg beinahe vergessen. Erst die vorliegende Publikation hat hier seit der 1. Auflage von 2003 eine Trendwende geschafft. Inzwischen wird Peter Browe unter die wichtigsten Liturgiewissenschaftler des 20. Jahrhunderts gezählt. Neben Josef Andreas Jungmann SJ (†1975) und Hans-Bernhard Meyer SJ (†2002) darf er sogar als einer der „Top Drei" der eucharistietheologischen Forschung gelten.
Bd. 1, 7. Aufl. 2019, 580 S., 39,90 €, br., ISBN 978-3-643-14396-9

LIT Verlag Berlin – Münster – Wien – Zürich – London
Auslieferung Deutschland / Österreich / Schweiz: siehe Impressumsseite